Offer Value
Enjoy Success

Improve and Promote Your Value Offering

Ron Pieper

Paperback ISBN: 978-1-7376968-0-3
eBook ISBN: 978-1-7376968-1-0

First Paperback Edition: August 2021

Blue Orchid Media
Virginia, United States of America

Submit any queries regarding this book directly to the author at
Ron.PieperJr@gmail.com

Table of Contents

Preface

I learned about value offering much later in life than I wish I had. I find that many people do. And I see many people who have yet to learn about it or perhaps are still amidst learning about it. Value offering is very important to each of us. It improves our potential for opportunities and success in anything we do whether it pertains to our careers, our hobbies, our families, our employees, our customers, anything. Is that not something we would like to know early in life?

Receiving opportunities and achieving success can be challenging. It often was for me in my early years. I am fortunate to be able to reflect on many wonderful opportunities and successes in my life. As I reflect on them, I can easily see where I was more successful once I started embracing this thing called *value offering*. Before understanding value offering and embracing it, my track record was less impressive. It was full of *learning opportunities*, as I like to call them tongue-in-cheek.

Over time I became comfortable in teaching value offering to people who worked for me and eventually I started helping many client audiences. Everyone has value to offer. Everyone. Sometimes we just need a little help seeing it. Sometimes we need to enhance it. I am writing this book as a way to reach more people like you in hopes that to some degree my experiences may help others in their life pursuits of opportunities and successes.

This book is a guide. In here I explain much about value offering and I guide you through a process to develop and leverage your value offering. You can use this book on your own or use it equally well in group settings. It is designed to be used either way.

Chapter 1

Value Offering

It Is Needed

Each of us wants something. We go through our entire lives wanting to accomplish, or to achieve, many things. From our earliest days we wanted to succeed doing something. We may not remember all of them, but we know we had plenty of wants in our early lives. That does not change as we age and enter school, start a career, form a family, or enter retirement. In fact, our wants tend to increase over time. What we want will also change during our lives, but what does not change is our desire to accomplish something. Sometimes those accomplishments are for ourselves and sometimes they will be for the benefit of others, and very often they will be for both. In other words, we like successes.

Whether it is a material object or something less tangible, we take actions to obtain that item and we expend a lot of time and effort doing so. Very little comes our way in the form of unsolicited gifts for which we put forth little or no effort. We have to plan, communicate with other people, schedule events, make decisions, be persistent, be patient, and much more. Each of us can easily remember achievements that were very challenging and some that came more easily when we were prepared. Sometimes we succeeded, sometimes we did not. People who prepare themselves can increase their likelihood of success.

I label achievements into two categories. The first are achievements that directly contribute to our own successes without relying on actions by other people. The second category are those achievements that involve other people, specifically influencing other people or contributing to successes for other people.

Practicing to run faster for that next 5K race or learning more about gardening so we have attractive yards are achievements we generally pursue for our own satisfaction. These contribute directly to our own success. We lace up and hit the track or the treadmill and, hopefully, our efforts develop more speed and stamina. We run faster and are more energetic – a success. We read a gardening magazine with valuable information about plants and fertilizers. Then we use that information to buy plants that are durable and colorful, and we know more about planting and feeding the plants so they grow well. These are examples of the first category of achievements where we put forth effort to improve our abilities because we wanted to do better for ourselves. In these scenarios, we achieved success by improving our athleticism and having a more attractive yard and did not rely on influencing other people.

The next category, and just as pertinent to this book, includes achievements we pursue that will influence other people to contribute to our successes or where these achievements contribute to someone else's successes. This occurs in all sorts of settings including our work place, clubs, family and friend networks, our neighborhoods, sports teams, school, you name it. Let us discuss this a bit.

For example, since you are knowledgeable on gardening and lawncare, and you are good at it, people ask you to help them with their gardens and pay you for your services. Perhaps this is now your second job, or your new career path or business. Your own achievement in developing this skillset influenced other people to contribute to more successes for yourself vis a vis additional income or a new line of work.

Or perhaps you just want to help people without expecting anything in return. You help your friend with her garden and she is very happy with the project, and now she does not have to hire an expensive gardening company. In these examples, someone other than yourself is either influenced to provide you with a subsequent success or is a happier person because of what you did for her, or both. You may be thinking that the two categories are linked in this scenario and you would be right in seeing it that way. This is often the case. By achieving your own success in become a gardening expert (the first category), you can be better at influencing other people and contributing to their own successes (the second category).

In the above scenario is your value offering. Your personal achievement in being really good at gardening influences someone to do something for you such as being a new customer for your business and/or provides success, happiness, cost savings, or something positive for that other person. Win Win!

To better understand value offering, let us review both words independently. A search in dictionaries and scholarly resources will yield a variety of definitions for "value" referring to worth, usefulness, desirability, importance, and more. I much prefer describing "value" in terms of "benefit" that something or some*one* offers. When I benefit from something, that thing has value for me. This definition removes a lot of subjectivity, thereby helping people discern actual value to themselves. For example, a coffee shop can offer a free drink if we buy two drinks (buy 2, get 1 free) and claim that has value for us. If I am alone and I only want to drink one cup of coffee, then spending the extra money for that second drink in order to get two additional drinks that I cannot or do not want to consume is not valuable to me. There is no benefit for me. (OK, OK, maybe a coffee example is a bad example given how much I love coffee, but I suspect you understand my point.) On the other hand, if three friends walk into that coffee shop together intending to buy three cups of coffee, then this 3-for-2 sale special has value for them. They benefit from this sale because they save money on a product (i.e., a free third cup of coffee) they were initially expecting to buy at full price.

With this coffee shop example, I want to demonstrate the importance of defining value in terms of benefit to someone. If you are achieving something just for yourself, such as more coffee for less money, then that someone is you. If you are trying to influence someone else with your achievements in knowing how to run a good coffee shop with good pricing, then the value you want to offer must yield a benefit to that other person. As the seller of that coffee, the value of the sales promotion is not for you. That value is for someone you want as a customer and having customers is a need for your business success. Those customers benefit because they save money and in turn you benefit because you have more business income and perhaps repeat customers. This all started by you having a value offering.

In our gardening scenario, the forming of value to provide benefit to another person can involve a lot. Your education and practice that makes you good at gardening are very important. You know which plants grow well in the type of soil that is in the garden. You know which plants grow well in the sun or in the shade. You know how to place plants to be decorative. You know the seasonal cycles of colorful blooms so that the gardens will have color for longer periods of time. You know you need to ask your customer about their preferences – roses or hostas, shrubs or flowers, tall or short, annuals or perennials. You know to ask for a timeframe or deadline for your project. You know to ask about budget and how to plan to perform the work within budget. You know that each customer will have different interests. Knowing all this may seem valuable, and technically it is, but actually doing well with all this knowledge to satisfy your customer provides the benefit and that is the full value that is important.

Having value is very important. (I will say this a lot. Because, well, it is very important…) Offering your value to someone and offering it in the right way is even more important. We need to inform people of our value and we need to do so in a way that compels them to appreciate and want that value. This is how we gain their support for something we want, such as having them as a customer or getting them to hire us after the job interview. Playing "I have a secret" is not the game to play when you want people to contribute to your success. "Your success" can refer to yourself, your business, your team, your family, and more.

Offering, in its simplest definition as a noun, is a *thing* you present. To be successful in your life with your value, this definition falls woefully short. Your

> **!**
> Offer value by
> ensuring benefit

offering needs to convey your value which in turn yields benefit. You may

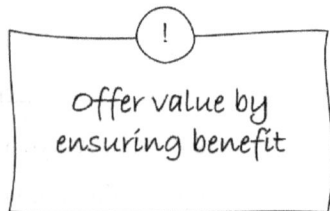

be talented at organizing files and tasks in a way that can help people operate more efficiently so that the business overall performs well, but if you just write on your resume that you can create folders and write To Do Lists I am pretty sure you will not get invited to many interviews. If the *thing* you offered was just a set of skill sets, nope not enough. Remember, think of *benefit* when you form and define your value and offer it in a way that compels people to want it.

What is it about being skilled at organizing files, information, task lists, and other office matters that is important for the other person to understand? Many, many people are good at this. Why are you better? Why should you get the job vice someone else? Identify the benefit. The benefit you offer with this skillset may be assurance the company will consistently comply with Government regulations and limit the risk of fines, law suits, or losing the business license. It may be enabling workers to meet deadlines so that services or products are delivered to customers on time which may entice those customers to be repeat customers whose money provides paychecks for the employees. It may be alleviating burden and frustration for the workforce because they will no longer spend a lot of time searching for missing records and information, and as a result the work climate may be more enjoyable. These benefits are what you may write in your resume as your offering - your value offering.

For my own clients, I define value offering as follows:

> *Value Offering is the benefit you will provide other people, that those other people want or need, and is presented in a way that compels them to accept your offer.*

I encourage you to write that definition down and place it where you will see it. Maybe on the office wall or on your desk.

As a consultant, I definitely need a good value offering. Actually, having a few value offerings is a good idea, but at least one that I can modify to satisfy differing prospective clients. My clients are diverse and so are their interests and needs and standards and expectations. What I offer one prospective client may not be satisfactory for another prospective client even though they may be seeking assistance on the same type of issue. Generally, the main focus of my consulting is to help business clients develop and implement ways to improve their businesses and to help individual clients to develop and implement ways to improve their value. I do not need to completely change my value offering each time, just tweak it a bit to be relevant for a particular client. I adapt. This adaptability, by the way, is part of my value offering. I recognize that there is no one-size-fits-all approach to helping all clients, so my value offering includes tailoring services for optimal performance in support of my diverse clients.

My value offering, as a consultant, is basically enabling clients to improve their potential for continued success and I do that by providing tailored consulting services. I will provide a couple examples to demonstrate this. (Note: In this book, I refrain from referring to the identities of my clients. Many of them expect me to protect their confidentiality since they are businesses and that means they do not want to disclose their activities to potential competitors.)

One of my business clients sought assistance in identifying ways to form his new company. He formed a company to provide information technology services that would include services for 24/7 help desks, designing new networks, hardware and software support (e.g., repairing laptops, installing printers, updating software applications), and various other services. He personally had a background in information technology services and I was quite impressed with the extent of his knowledge in this area. He wanted his company to provide services to larger companies and Government customers where he envisioned sizeable business opportunities. He was a former senior federal government employee with an information technology services job, so he was familiar with that customer and he also had ideas on how he could help them as a new business owner. He was also well aware of the information technology needs of larger companies because many of them had been service providers supporting him in his government position.

So, Ryan (I will use this pseudonym for this example) had preferences for the portfolio of services he wanted to provide based on his own areas of expertise and experience. He had a lot of expertise, but he was not an expert on everything. And that was fine, since no one is an expert on all information technology topics – there is a lot out there. Information technology services are numerous, complex, and dynamic as technology rapidly changes. He was knowledgeable of technology challenges he witnessed in his previous place of employment and with challenges he heard about from colleagues in other government offices. He had an idea of what services he wanted to provide and ideas for solving some specific customer issues. This was a great start, yet only a partial start.

What help was he seeking from a consultant? He wanted someone to help him develop his business strategy and plan. For those of you who own or manage businesses, you know how extensive this can be. For the rest of you, trust me, this is a big project. I spent some time learning more about Ryan's expertise, his goals for his business, his vision, his standards and expectations, and much more. I needed to know what I had to work with and what may be missing. I then proceeded to inform him of what I can and would do for him should he hire me as his consultant.

I told Ryan that I would assist him with developing a framework for his business that would set his business up for enduring success. I offered my expertise in facilitating ideation (i.e., working with him and his team to identify ideas and solutions for this consulting project), strategizing and planning for businesses, marketing, organization and team development. I offered my responsiveness, reliability, and partnership. I actually have only modest knowledge of information technology, certainly not to the extent of Ryan's knowledge. Fortunately, this project did not need a consultant with that type of expertise. And where I may want to incorporate information technology expertise, Ryan could certainly contribute.

That business framework with which I would assist in developing would include many things:

1. *A business strategy and business plan.* These would identify business goals, processes and procedures for operations, organization structure, workforce requirements (i.e., type of expertise, size), professional development program for continuous employee training, employee and company certifications for this highly technical line of business, prioritization of markets based on their revenue potential (budgets, needs for information technology services), advertising strategy, financial planning, means of periodically assessing or measuring the business for continuous improvement, and much more.

2. *Market analysis and prioritization.* (This is actually a part of most business plans, yet I like to initially break it out as a dedicated project to ensure it receives additional focus.) This involved researching multiple potential markets such as specific departments in the federal Government, large retail companies and manufacturing companies, service provider companies, and others. Each market has varying needs for information technology services and varying budgets to purchase them, so analyzing them is necessary.

3. *Analysis of competition.* This involved researching and assessing his competitors. The information technology industry is highly competitive because there are so many companies and there is a very high consumer demand. This analysis should guide him on how to improve his own offering in order to compete.

4. *Marketing.* Some items included in marketing are brand development, price models, and advertising.

5. *Organization development.* We would define how his business would be organized in terms of teams and roles, skill set requirements, lines of authority, and communications channels.

6. *Resources.* His business was going to need its own information technology such as computers, internet resources, email accounts, a customer relations management system; office space; training resources; advertising services; a financial management system; a web site; and much more.

7. *Legal stuff.* Insurance, workforce reporting, business name registration, tax reporting, etc.

8. *More and more and more.* The above list is only a start on this major project.

So what was my value offering? For Ryan, I would reliably partner with him to form a business framework that would maximize his business potential, that would mitigate risks, and that would be enduring. I would provide significant relevant expertise that would assure an optimal final product. I would do so at a fair cost and finish the project on time.

I have many types of clients and the way I approach each project differs. My value offering may even be modified. For example, some of my clients have been Government offices. They, too, need a strategy and plan on how they will operate in support of their many customers, but they did not need to consider making profits and in many cases they do not need to search for customers. (Some Government offices do, though.)

One such government client provided information technology services for other Government offices within its agency. (Offices like this are often titled Office of the Chief Information Officer.) I assisted this office in forming their strategy and plan for supporting their agency. This project included all the same components I provided to Ryan in my previous example, except that this client obviously was not interested in having paying customers. So, they did not have to identify and prioritize customers; their customers were already known and they were all the other offices in the agency. Yet this client still needed to organize its team, obtain and manage resources, engage customers to obtain their requirements, administer training, satisfy regulatory and legal requirements such as reporting and security, and much more just like Ryan needed to do.

My value offering was very similar, only slightly modified. I would reliably partner with my client to form an operational framework that would maximize their customer service potential, mitigate risks, and be enduring. I would provide significant relevant expertise that would assure an optimal final product. I would do so at a fair cost and finish the project on time.

While I speak about my value offering for these two clients, the end result was assistance for both clients (a business and a Government office) to form and deliver on their own value offerings for their customers (other businesses, Government offices, and individuals). By having sound business and operational frameworks in place as I described, they were able to provide a good value offering to their customers.

Why is value offering important? A value offering, a good one, makes you highly competitive for selection and contributes to your success in your current role. Your value offering is intended to provide desirable value to your audience, be they clients, hiring managers, customers, employees, family and friends, or others. It is intended to be more attractive to your target audience than what your competitors offer, such that you are the person who is selected for that new role or the business selected as a new customer's favorite. When only one person can be selected, we need to be better than the person who comes in second place. Succeeding in your current role means you are accomplishing your assigned duties and contributing to your team's successes.

While I speak much to the importance of a value offering, a value offering must also be real. You must be able to deliver on it. Recall my use of "reliably" in my value offering? Reliability such as timeliness, credibility, trustworthiness, availability, and other valuable traits are critical components of a good value offering. Beyond the obvious ethics of this point, you risk losing future pursuits when a dissatisfied customer or employee has only negative reviews to provide on your performance.   Offer value, then deliver value on your offer.

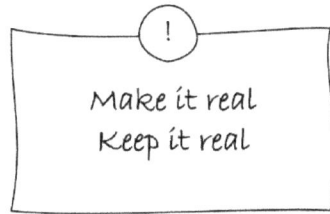

> !
> Make it real
> Keep it real

In order to influence other people to select us, we must be able to give them what they want. If we cannot give them what they want, we will not be selected for what they want. It is that simple. No new job, no promotion, no position on the ball team, no customer, no laughs at the Dad jokes. When we are selected and we are good at what that other person wants, we set ourselves up for more success. That customer comes back to buy more from your business and tells their friends to visit your business. That new job gives you more skills and experience that can lead to the next and, hopefully, better job. Even if you are not seeking additional future opportunities, being good at what you do today can help you keep that position and help you help your team. That initial success achieved by delivering on your value offering can lead to continued success and additional successes. Having a good value offering is extraordinarily important.

Imagine sitting in a job interview. You want that position as a team manager for a team of account managers at a medical billing services company. You are being interviewed by Alicia. She is the Vice President of Operations for the company and you would work directly for her, as does the other account team managers. You have experience working on medical billing teams in processing bills and payments, using various systems to record transactions, and in customer communications. You believe you are now ready for a role as a team manager.

This is not a position in which you will only process billing transactions like you do in your current position, though. You will be responsible for the well-being and performance of other people. During the interview, Alicia wants to know how you will ensure each person on your team meets performance standards, how you will protect sensitive information and comply with medical community regulations such as those associated with HIPAA (Health Insurance Portability and Accountability Act), how you will promote a positive work climate, how you would screen prospective employees for your team, how you will manage employees struggling with their performance, how you would manage violence or sexual harassment in the work place, how you would ensure work is accomplished when people are on vacation or when positions are vacated by someone's resignation, and how you would forecast operational performance of the business in view of your team's performance. I am certain this is just a small sample of the questions and topics that may be covered in such an interview. So, what are your answers? In other words, in addition to the detailed approaches you have to offer, what is your value offering? Are you ready to present that and answer Alicia's tough yet important questions? A series of "uhhhh", "well...", "ummm", "I guess I would..." will likely lead to a short interview.

You need to be ready. For the above scenario, anticipate the line of questioning. You may not know the specific questions Alicia will ask, but you ought to expect what may be of interest to her which will be the topics her questions will address. In fact, if you are seeking a position as a team manager, you should be interested in much the same things that are of interest to Alicia. You may become her new manager. Your value offering is not just ensuring accurate processing of billing transactions. You are doing that now in your current position. Your value offering for a manager position needs to speak to team performance, caring for people, and contributing to the success of the business. When you need to influence other people in your pursuit of opportunities, you need a good value offering.

You can and I am certain you will form a winning value offering. You likely already have many valuable skills and knowledge. You may have the beginnings of a good value offering already, perhaps one that was good for another purpose and you just need to improve upon it. You should not feel like you are starting from scratch. You definitely have value today and I assume you are interested in this topic given you are reading this book. In the following chapters I hope to provide useful assistance to you as you form that winning value offering. We are on the path to great success!

- Ponder Page -

Chapter 2

Identify Your Objectives

How do we form and maintain a winning value offering? This requires some effort, but it need not be daunting. It requires research, analysis, training, practice, and more that is well within your ability to accomplish. And a well-defined process will help. No worries, the process is easy to understand and easy to follow. And it works. My intent with this book is to help you in forming and maintaining winning value offerings and that includes providing you with a process and some guidance.

Look at this like taking a trip. There is a specific location you seek as your endpoint and you plan your trip to arrive there. We consider what we need in order to get there and we consider what we will need while we are there. We could simply stroll out of the house with a desire to arrive at the beach or the mountains across country, but we may not have a good experience trying to get there without a plan for the route, a budget, a schedule, hotel reservations, or changes of clothes and other supplies. Notice I said "trying" to get there. Without a good plan derived from a good planning process, we may not arrive at our destination. Now, beach and mountain vacations may seem more exciting than value offerings – gasp! – but the metaphor is apt.

The process for forming your value offering similarly begins with understanding what you want to get out of having a value offering. In other words,

> !
> What do you want?
> Now tell yourself!

where do you want to end up or what do you want to achieve. We start at the end so to speak. This is typically the most effective approach to any

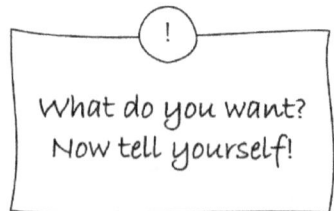

planning, but unfortunately many people are not aware of this. Except you of course, you know now. Start by identifying where you want to be, then plan on what you need to do now and how to do it to get to your destination. Remember, your value offering is part of the plan to arriving at your destination.

We will apply a six-step process which I portray on the following page. Each step is defined to achieve specific milestones for your value offerings. For this Chapter, we will discuss Step 1 "Identify Objectives".

Identify Objectives **YOU ARE HERE**	This is what you want to achieve for which a value offering will help.
Analysis of Target Audience	Who needs to be influenced and how can they be influenced. What's important to them?
Defining Personal Value Offering	This is the value you will offer. It can be single or multi-faceted.
Developing Your Value Offering	Obtaining knowledge, skills, resources, and more to create your value offering.
It's Show Time!	Promote your value offering to your target audience.
Continuous Value	We should continuously improve.

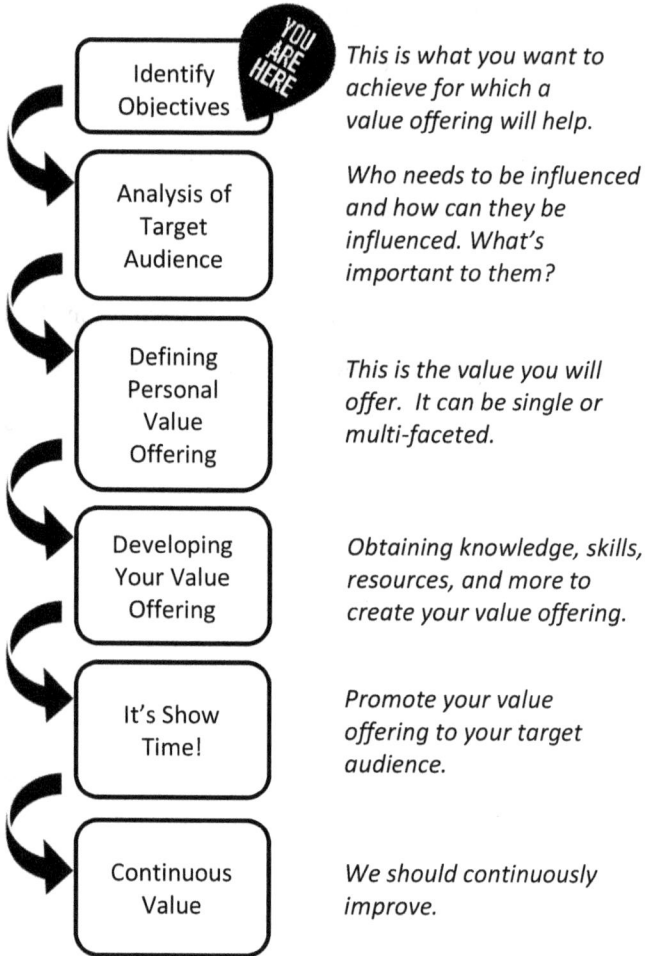

Identifying our objective may seem an easy thing to do. It can be easy to get it right. It can also be easy to get it wrong. Please, be very diligent in identifying your objective. This is the first step on your journey and you need to step in the right direction. Because of the importance of this step, we are going to take some time to cover it thoroughly.

In identifying your objective, be specific. Start by identifying the high-level objective like getting that job for which you are interviewing, then decide on the detailed objectives about that job like desired salary, work location, or other specifics that are important to you. Identifying that high level objective may be easy because it is obvious to you. To identify the detailed objectives requires additional thought. It requires us to reflect on what is important to us and what we want. It is the detail of what we intend to achieve that typically impacts our daily lives, not just the high-level objective alone.

You got a job as Veterinarian Assistant that had a job announcement stating the employee would help the Veterinarian with clinic operations. You were looking forward to working directly for the Veterinarian and caring for your soon-to-be customers' pets. You like animals. But you identified your objective simply as getting the job and failed to consider the details of what the job would actually entail in comparison to what you wanted out of the job. You assumed the job entailed working with animals. The veterinarian was considering many duties she needed someone to perform, and she had not yet decided on specifically which ones would be performed by the new employee. She did not speak untruthfully when she said that everyone at the clinic was part of a team that cared about pets and helped in some way with the clinic taking care of those pets. But, when you started your job you discovered the veterinarian decided you would help her with her paperwork – record keeping and billing clients – and that was about it. This is very important work and many people like it (thankfully!), but it is not what you wanted to do. But wait, what about actually taking care of the pets did you want to do? Technically, your role in tending to the paperwork, as long as you did it well, contributes to how well the team - you are a part of the team now – will be able to care for the pets. But you wanted to groom them, walk them, and other hands-on services. So, you actually are helping the pets in the administrative role, just not in ways you had hoped to help.

You missed an opportunity in the interview to fully express your interests (i.e., your detailed objectives) and abilities, and the Veterinarian chose a job description for you based on what she thought you could best manage. You did not hone in on your detailed objective of working directly with animals and as a result you did not speak to that during the interview. In the Veterinarian's mind, you were still going to help with pets. It just would not be hands-on touchy-cuddly with them. What was important to you? Maybe it *was* the paperwork and you would likely be very happy with the turn-out. Maybe it was directly helping with the animals, in which case you needed to mention this and convince the veterinarian that you would be very good at it. Always work with details.

I find the most effective way to help clients with this first step is to review many scenarios and then facilitate an exercise. The exercise is at the end of this chapter and can be used for yourself or for a group. I am going to use multiple scenarios to provide diverse settings and circumstances. I am going to practice what I teach – working with details. Again, as we review these scenarios, remember that we need to identify our high-level objective then define the specifics we want with that objective.

For our first scenario, let us say that you want to sell baked goodies. These include cookies, cakes, and other sweet treats. You love baking and you are really good at it. You bake for friends and they always ask for more of your apple crustadas, snickerdoodles, and cinnamon-sugar cream puffs. You have given some thought about doing this as a business. Maybe you set up your own shop open to the public. Maybe you only set up a kitchen for your baking and sell just to businesses. I heard you preferred to sell to businesses. This business model would allow you to focus on your baking which is truly what you enjoy and avoid running a larger business where you would have to deal with leasing, building maintenance, and a lot of expenses in order to sell directly to the public. You may consider setting up a bakery that would be open to the public later after you have had time to perfect your products and save some investment money.

The area around you has a few coffee shops and a ton of restaurants of all types and sizes. Some of the coffee shops sell sweets, yet you notice the selections are minimal and you also notice customers looking at them with marginal interest. Some buy, some do not. You can tell that the shops buy from a commercial supplier and that means that wedge of lemon pound cake is several days or even weeks old, was probably frozen, and likely has additives we would rather not consume. Many restaurants sell commercially-supplied boxed desserts, too, and their menu has only three options that never change.

You also begin thinking about those office meetings and the boxes of frosted donuts. Donuts are fun, some people like donuts. But at every meeting? Oh, and that day when someone brought a small bag of crunchy cookies they bought from the grocery store. No, just no. But heyyyyyy, gatherings of people…hmmm. Hungry people gather for many things. Conferences, birthday parties, quinceanos, wedding anniversaries, retirement parties, high school graduations, baby showers, grand opening of your neighbor's new pool and BBQ fire pit. Sounds like another customer demographic.

How would you define your high-level objective? Tip: Identify multiple high-level objectives. Sometimes our first thought is the right one. Sometimes, though, it can be quite useful to consider multiple options. We may select one of the others or combine bits and pieces of them to form a completely alternate option. Write down the high-level objectives without refining them. Let your thoughts flow freely like brainstorming. This is not the point where we filter or refine our thoughts. We will do that later as we work the details.

Here are some high-level objectives that come to mind for me.

1. Sell baked goods, sweet and savory, to the public in caterer-like style.
2. Sell baked goods to local businesses.
3. Test baked goods for sales potential at our own bakery to be set up later.
4. Sell cakes and cookies.

How does your list of high-level objectives compare to my list? My list is not comprehensive. If you have something different than I do, it may be perfectly fine. In fact, they may be much better. If you said something like "Sell stuff", you may want to cross that one out. That is too broad. "Sell baked goods" may also be too broad. "Baked goods" can include a ham or roasted vegetables, but you want to sell the sweet stuff. Did you refer to making money? Something like, make enough money selling cookies to pay my bills and save for that bakery storefront. That would be fine.

I like to add more information in my high-level objectives to guide where I go with defining the eventual detailed objectives. You see that for a couple of my high-level objectives I referred to "local businesses" and "public". I do that because the detailed objectives may be different based on the customer set.

To complete this scenario, I am going to select my second high-level objective: Sell baked goods to local businesses like those coffee shops. Let's identify the detailed objectives for this. How do we start? We start by understanding influencers. These are things that influence... They include things like our wants and interests, our abilities, our resources, and the type of pursuit itself (e.g., food business). Do we want to make a lot of money or just have fun? Do we like sweet or savory baked goods, or both? Do we prefer to make commonly known items like oatmeal cookies and chocolate cupcakes, or do we like to live on the edge and make petit fours, traditional Italian cheesecakes, and Quiche Lorraine. (My answer is "yes" to all of those goodies by the way.) What do we currently make very well? What would we like to make well and just need some practice? How much oven space do we have, meaning how much can we bake each day? How much refrigerator space do we have available to store items that need to be chilled, including ingredients for recipes and the final products? How far are we willing to drive to deliver our goods? How much time do we have to prepare the goods and deliver them? What are the regulations and laws regarding preparing food items for sale to the public? What licenses and permits do we need to own and operate a business? What insurance do we need? And on and on and on… These matters and others have an influence on us and our decision.

Do not place restrictions on yourself when identifying your objectives. Do not get in your own way. To achieve an objective, we must have an objective. In your planning, when you discover influencers that appear like challenges, do not see them as road blocks. Consider them more like bumps in the road and acknowledge the progress you make every time you pass over one. See this as something to resolve. I refer to these as *influencers*. Some may only be slightly challenging. Admittedly, some may be very hard to overcome. The point is to work towards overcoming these challenging influencers and you will overcome many, if not all, of them.

Influencers have a direct impact on our potential in achieving our objectives. Impact can be negative or positive. It is important to understand this so we can leverage them where they are good and mitigate them where they are not good. For example, if we are really good at making scones, we may want our objective to become the supplier of large quantities of scones to local coffee shops. One influencer will be our cooking capacity. If we do not have a lot of oven space to cook large quantities of scones, we will be challenged in achieving our objective. In this case we may choose to change our objective to something else or mitigate the challenge by buying another oven, probably a large oven, so we can keep our preferred objective. If we have plenty of ovens, then our cooking capacity is a positive influencer. This, too, will influence our objectives.

Examples of other influencers could be your ability to make pastries better than you make cakes, your bakery's proximity to your target customers, your interests in one product over another, and the size of bakery your finances will support.

This research and preparation are often referred to as "business planning" and that is a topic, a very important topic, that falls outside of the scope of this book. It warrants its own study because it can be quite extensive. For this book on value offering we will assume that business planning is working in concert with our work on forming our value offering. By the way, your value offering is a component of your business plan.

For this scenario, here are some detailed objectives I suggest we consider. I am going to assume for the convenience of this demonstration that we have sufficient resources and skills for our business interest.

1. Be the sole supplier of baked goods for each of the three locally owned coffee shops. (I recommend stating the names of the business for clarity.)
2. Become the sole supplier of desserts for at least four locally owned restaurants.
3. Gain favorable recognition to support future growth.
4. Supply customers daily/maintain customer daily demand.
5. Obtain customer demand for a variety of baked goods.

What detailed objectives do you have to add to this list? Did you identify different detailed objectives? Are there any of mine you would remove? Detailed objectives need to be useful to *you* in developing *your* value offering. Reminder: Your value offering is part of your business plan because of its importance to increasing your potential of success.

Allow me to explain my reasoning for selecting this initial list of detailed objectives.

1. *Be the sole supplier of baked goods for each of the three locally owned coffee shops.* This is detailed because it refers to being the sole supplier for a specific number of a specific type of customer. If you want to be these coffee shops' sole supplier, then you need to have an offering that provides them confidence that you can contribute to their business successes better than anyone else. That may include providing better baked goods, being timely with your shipments, providing

money-back guarantees, partnering in creative ways to grow business together, and much more.

You wanting to sell to all coffee shops may conger concerns by the coffee shop owners about competition among the coffee shops or concerns about your ability to operate your brand new business at that larger scale. But, you have an opportunity to impress upon these three coffee shop owners that you can contribute to their success. By gaining a loyal customer base for your baked goods that are sold at one of the coffee shops, those customers may talk about your baked goods to their friends who live closer to a different coffee shop. Those friends visit that other coffee shop and buy your baked goods and you may eventually grow from there. You may also provide different goodies to each coffee shop so the shops are still individualized, yet your labeling still draws loyal customers.

I am not suggesting that it would be a poor decision to target all coffee shops. I am narrowing my objective for the sake of this learning scenario.

Specifying coffee shops as a target customer is valuable because this may guide you in selecting the baked goods you would offer and your pricing for those items. We likely would not sell many full-size cakes at coffee shops because customers typically need the convenience of hand-held products. They walk away with a cup of coffee in one hand and a cinnamon glazed scone in the other. And coffee shop customers wanting a take-away order to enjoy while driving are more likely to pay $1.50 for that jumbo peanut butter cookie with strawberry jam baked in the center than $15 for that six inch high nine inch wide German chocolate cake. You also selected coffee shops because you know that they have many customers who want some goodies to go with their coffee, and their customers will be your customers.

2. *Become the sole supplier of desserts for at least four locally owned restaurants.* The reason for identifying this detailed objective of being the sole supplier for a specific number of restaurants is essentially the same as described above for coffee shops. Selecting an additional form of business provides an opportunity to sell a wider selection of baked goods which can generate additional revenue. For dine-in restaurants, you can now more easily sell those large German chocolate cakes for which people would sit and use a fork. Additionally, by having some diversity in customers, over time you may discover that one type of customer is more or less profitable for you than another type of customer. By having multiple customers, you will increase your odds of having some who are profitable to you.

3. *Gain favorable recognition to support future growth.* The importance of favorable recognition cannot be overstated. It

is absolutely critical for your success. We are talking about favorable brand recognition in a broad sense – highly desirable products, good pricing, reliable delivery, cordial and fair business practices, good person-to-person chemistry, etc.

I suspect each of you reading this book recognizes that your customers will need to like your products. It is also important for them to like your overall business to include your customer service and even yourself. Customers are more likely to continue buying from you when they like you and your product line. Yet, you also need to expand recognition of your baked goods, your business, and yourself to other potential customers. Your coffee shop and restaurant owners may speak favorably about your products on their websites and social media pages to their friends and other business owners. Do not consider the coffee shop and restaurant owners as your only customers by the way. They sell your baked goods to their customers. If their customers did not buy your baked goods, those coffee shop and restaurant owners won't either. Their customers need to like your baked goods more than those business owners do. Their customers are your customers and initial source of the income stream.

4. *Supply customers daily/maintain daily customer demand.* This is important because your brand includes fresh baked goods. Have you ever eaten a 2-day old donut? If you have, please deny it. Dry, greasy, stale, yuk.

You know that in order to have a successful business selling baked goods, you need to provide your goods freshly baked. This means same-day, or at least within the past few hours from baking late last night to this morning's sale. I always ask about the age of food in display cases. In addition to providing their customers with freshly baked goods, we want our coffee shop and restaurant owners to receive our baked goods daily because we may not have the ability nor interest in costly storage. The coffee shop and restaurant owners may not be able to store multi-day stock either. Daily shipments can fit on your counter, in your delivery vehicle, and in their display cases.

5. *Obtain customer demand for a variety of baked goods.* Have you ever heard the cliché "one trick pony"? When the pony can only do one thing, it is no longer entertaining and does not keep the crowd. You may make the best blueberry turnover and first-time customers push people out of the way to fight over them. But, if that is the only thing you try to sell each day, those initial customers can tire of them. People like variety. Generally, we get bored with the same-o same-o each day.

You also would miss out on those other customers who do not like blueberry turnovers and would really like to buy your chocolate cream-filled hand pies. We want our coffee shop and restaurant owners to order and stock a variety of our baked goods. This is not to say that our customers should not stock some of the same items day-to-day. There will be *best sellers* and the display inventory should routinely include them, and balanced with a few items that change occasionally to provide variety. This increases their sales potential which is your sales potential. That coffee shop owner who understands this is also the customer you want. This is a sign that they understand how to be successful with their business and that can equate to your long-term success. You also now know that our value offering of a variety of baked goods will be in demand.

For our second scenario, we work with a company that provides information technology services. We help customers with hardware and software installation, database management, security, information management, troubleshooting and maintenance, and trouble ticket management. There are many information technology services beyond these. It seems this line of work is changing often with rapid changes in technologies and customer requirements. Many of the skill sets endure yet evolve in face of advances in hardware and software and continuous education. These skills can include network engineering, software development, testing and evaluation, configuration management, service desk management, cyber security, and much more.

One day the Chief Operations Officer wanted to identify additional services the company could provide to improve its business potential. She promulgated an email in which she invited the Vice Presidents and Directors to suggest ideas.

You have experience with business operations. You are involved in a portion of them now and may have managed business operations at other companies. Maybe you studied marketing in college even though it was your second choice elective class. With your experience you understand that this initiative warrants some good rigor if it has much of a chance of succeeding, and in this you see an opportunity for yourself. As they say, an opportunity to excel.

The opportunity you recognize is to directly assist the COO with her initiative in a formal role. In doing so you hope to contribute even more to this initiative than just ideation. (While my presentation throughout this book heavily focuses on ways to benefit you which can seem unduly self-serving, please know by obtaining opportunities like this and by improving your performance ability that your team can benefit as well. Benefiting the team is always important.) This opportunity of directly helping the COO may also provide you valuable exposure to people who may become interested in affording you additional opportunities such as new roles and positions in the company. At minimum, you could gain experience that improves your skill set for your current position – an improvement to your current value offering - and this experience can be documented in your resume for that next job. There are a lot of potential wins for people who step up to embrace teamwork like this.

How would you define the high-level objective? The high-level objective may be defined as establishing a leadership position for the COO's project, one that you hope to fill. The high-level objective may be to gain recognition from the COO for your readiness to contribute significantly to teamwork, and she may recall this in the future when she is looking for a new team leader. I am going to focus on an interest in establishing and performing a leading role for this scenario.

Now, we need to identify the detailed objectives to pursue in our conversation with the COO. If we just recommend to the COO that she form a position for this project (our high-level objective) and we stopped the conversation there, we may not have much of a chance of being selected. She needs to know you are interested in that leadership role and what you intend to do with the role and how the company is going to benefit from your leadership. When you are speaking with her, you do not want her thinking: "Hey, I know just the right person", and then she picks up the phone to call someone else.

Remember to be guided by your interest in having the position, by your abilities, and by what you know should be incorporated into the effort to identify additional services for the company to sell. Recall that you came up with this idea for a leadership position because you recognize that some rigor is needed for the COO's initiative. From my experience in helping clients with brand development – that is the term for creating and improving brand such as adding new services – I have some insight into what this effort will entail. You may have some experience in this area as well. Reflect on your experience and incorporate it into this process.

To help demonstrate how we would identify detailed objectives with this information technology company scenario, I list a few items below that would likely be incorporated into the COO's project. Your detailed objectives may eventually be formed based on an understanding of these potential project components. These components are the details of the project that may influence your objectives. This is just a sampling of what you would consider in the real-world. Give thought to anything you may add to this list or modify.

1. *Market research.* The company needs to analyze and assess potential markets and even specific customers. "Markets" are generally demographics like finance industry, retail industry, people who live in New York, et al. By "specific customers" I mean individual paying customers like the local trucking company that wants to provide all their drivers with laptops and email accounts. We would consider their problems that information technology services could resolve. Perhaps you know of a lot of companies that would benefit from video conferencing systems because they want to interact better with their own customers and employees around the country, or because they want to increase the amount their employees can telework on the road or at their homes. You may know some warehousing companies that need better ways to inventory and track their vast amount of stock.

2. *Research into additional education and industry certifications for the company's employees.* These can be very costly, yet often

necessary to ensure the workforce has the proper skill sets. There are industry certifications for companies, too.

3. *Workforce input.* Input should be obtained from across the company. With diversity in roles comes diversity in ideas and that is a strength. The technicians who work on-site at a customer's location personally see and hear about the customers' problems. The customers may be expressing an interest in services your company does not currently provide. At the technician level is where great ideas exist and smart managers leverage that knowledge.

The Human Resource Officer should research the availability and salary expectations of a workforce that would perform new services. We must ensure that there are people we can eventually hire, or at least enough of people we can train.

The Chief Financial Officer needs to identify the potential cost of adding new services, and forecast revenue and profit potential.

There are other matters to consider such as organizational structure for new people to provide new services (i.e., forming a new team or assigning new people to existing teams, using existing managers or hiring another manager), organization of new company operations, changes to office space or additions, and advertising to name a few. There are multiple people in the company with areas of responsibility pertinent to this project and those people should be considered for their expertise and decision-making authorities.

4. *Duration of the project and formation of interim milestones.* There needs to be a deadline for completing this project and there should be interim reporting of progress.

You have your high-level objective, you gathered some additional information, and identified people who you believe should be involved. This information and the people are influencers to consider in identifying your detailed objectives. What detailed objectives do you envision for yourself in this scenario? Again, you will eventually form your value offering in view of some or all of your detailed objectives. The following may be a good start:

1. *Obtain support from the COO in specifying the outcomes of this project.* Both of you will have interests, and so may others in the company. You need to know the COO's expectations for you so you can plan your operation and effectively guide your team. Your value offering you will eventually present may include a thorough understanding of what is important for achieving the COO's expectations. By asking this question, you set yourself up to refine your value offering.

2. *Define the duration of the project with specific start and end dates.* Your value offering may include your reliability in

meeting project deadlines. With the COO having a specified timeline for the project, she will want to know that you can manage time and achieve project milestones within deadlines.

3. *Obtain support for establishing a team.* You know that this is not a one-person project. You need help. Based on what I previously mentioned, perhaps the team can consist of some front-line managers, the Chief Financial Officer, the Human Resources Officer, technicians, business analysts who can research markets, and some others. We do not want a large team because it can be difficult to manage for a project like this. Yet you want enough people who can contribute useful experience and expertise. You will need to convince the COO that all these people are essential to this project. Your value offering may include your ability to manage matrixed teams and your good relationships with the people who may work on your team.

4. *Obtain support from managers for their technicians to spend some time on this team.* This will not likely be a full-time project for anyone, but each hour they spend on this project is an hour not supporting a paying customer. Managers will be justified in their concerns about their employees spending time away from their primary jobs to help with this project. Do not to forget that your own manager will need to support you taking on this role, too. This is an instance where your

ability to manage matrixed teams comprised of part-time members would be a good value offering.

5. *Obtain support from the COO for you to write the final report.* A well written report that conveys credible ways for the company to be profitable that has your name on it goes a long way to obtaining due recognition. You and the COO should define the format and content of the report beforehand. She can still present the report to her boss. Your value offering may be your ability to achieve desired outcomes for your projects and prepare top quality reports.

6. *Obtain support for a budget if you expect there to be any costs.* Some employees on your team may have to support you beyond their normal work schedules and perhaps they are entitled to overtime pay. Some companies track expenses per project and specific function, and they form individual budgets for this. A research firm may be hired to conduct the market research. A consultant may be hired who has done this before. You may want to consider a value offering in efficiently managing company resources to include the time and money spent by your team.

The preceding scenarios should help you understand the importance of how objectives should be defined and in how to define them. Remember, start by identifying what you want to get out of your pursuit and that may suffice as your high-level objective. This is often too general though, so consider refining it to ensure you are guiding yourself in the right direction. Consider potential influencers that can positively or negatively affect your potential for success. Then, consider those influencers and identify your detailed objectives. These will help you define your eventual value offering and set up your pursuit for success.

Identifying objectives is easy to understand and usually quite easy to accomplish. Advising on it, though, can be tricky. While the process is the same for any situation, each situation has different circumstances and eventually different objectives. Even facing the same situation, say applying for the same job, each person can have different interests in the outcome and, therefore, different objectives than the next person. I am going to briefly introduce a few more scenarios below to show how objectives may be defined in differing situations.

High-Level Objective: Seeking a position on a sports team.
Detailed Objectives:
- ➢ Obtain an offense position on the Paniolos soccer team.
- ➢ Obtain Center Forward position.
- ➢ Obtain back-up position as Second Striker or Attacking Midfielder

Note: With these being your detailed objectives, you may be guided to form a value offering of talent in playing offense and your ability to excel at multiple field positions.

High-Level Objective: Increase revenue for your home services business.

Detailed Objectives:

> ➤ Increase revenue by 15% within 60 days.
>
> ➤ Obtain 10 new house cleaning customers in 30 days, and sign annual service contracts
>
> ➤ Obtain 10 new lawn care customers in 30 days, and sign annual service contracts
>
> ➤ Identify services in demand by homeowners that may not be offered by other home services businesses. You may add these services to your company's portfolio.
>
> ➤ Identify the prices homeowners are paying your competitors. This helps assess your pricing model.
>
> ➤ Identify the services offered by your competitors that are in demand. You may add more services to your portfolio.
>
> ➤ Maintain at least 90% retention of current customers.

Note: With these being your detailed objectives, you would form your value offering to be attractive to homeowners needing cleaning services and homeowners who want a good looking yard every day. That may include shampooing carpets and degreasing stoves rather than just wiping down counters. It may include spraying plants to kill pests rather than just cutting grass.

High-Level Objective: Expand your advertising consulting business to new markets.

Detailed Objectives:
- ➤ Obtain three new clients in the energy manufacturing industry
- ➤ Obtain five new clients in the cyber security industry
- ➤ Obtain consulting schedules with new clients commencing within 90 days and lasting for at least 6 months each.
- ➤ Identify the services provided by competitors consulting in these new markets and their pricing.
- ➤ Achieve 10% growth in revenue with new clients over the next year.

High-Level Objective: Obtain a leadership position for a non-profit organization.

Detailed Objectives:
- ➤ Obtain the position with a non-profit organization near my location, within 30 miles.
- ➤ Obtain the position with a non-profit organization supporting children's education.
- ➤ Obtain a position that will require no more than 20 hours of service each month. Exceptions permitted for special events.
- ➤ Obtain a position coordinating volunteers or volunteer activities, business development, or advertising.

Now let us apply this process to a situation you may be facing. Apply this process to identify your high-level objective, the influencers you need to consider, and then your detailed objectives. Identifying objectives is an important early step. In later chapters we will discuss how to form a value offering guided by the high-level objective and the detailed objectives you identify.

Help others with this as well. If you have a team or if you are a consultant with clients, teach this process and guide them. I recommend demonstrating the application of this process on multiple scenarios to help them understand. Then guide them through applying the process to their own situations.

Below is a form that can help. Feel free to make copies of it. (Permission granted by me, the holder of the copyright.) This format works well on a dry-erase board for groups.

My High-Level Objective	
My Detailed Objectives	Influencers Upon My Objectives

- Ponder Page -

Chapter 3

What Are They Thinking?

We are still laying the ground work for crafting our value offering as we pursue our objectives. By this point of the process we would have given much thought and formed many good initial ideas. Now, we need to mature our understanding of the landscape so to speak. We need to understand the circumstances we may encounter in our efforts to obtain our objectives. For example, we may have selected to produce a podcast series on the topic of relaxation techniques for mental health with the objective of helping many stressed people. We now need to identify the answer, or answers, to the question: What is important to our target audience in terms of how they will decide to let us help them?

In identifying our objectives we formed an understanding of the scope of our pursuit. Our pursuit is more than just a job interview, starting a new business, increasing customers, or forming a podcast script. We are starting to understand the decisions, the work, and the resources involved in the pursuit of our objectives. Understanding the scope of our pursuit is important to being in synch with our target audience. This begins to prepare us to connect our pursuit and our target audience. The next step is to understand our target audience so we can truly connect the two.

Step	Description
Identify Objectives	*This is what you want to achieve for which a value offering will help.*
Analysis of Target Audience **YOU ARE HERE**	*Who needs to be influenced and how can they be influenced. What's important to them?*
Defining Personal Value Offering	*This is the value you will offer. It can be single or multi-faceted.*
Developing Your Value Offering	*Obtaining knowledge, skills, resources, and more to create your value offering.*
It's Show Time!	*Promote your value offering to your target audience.*
Continuous Value	*We should continuously improve.*

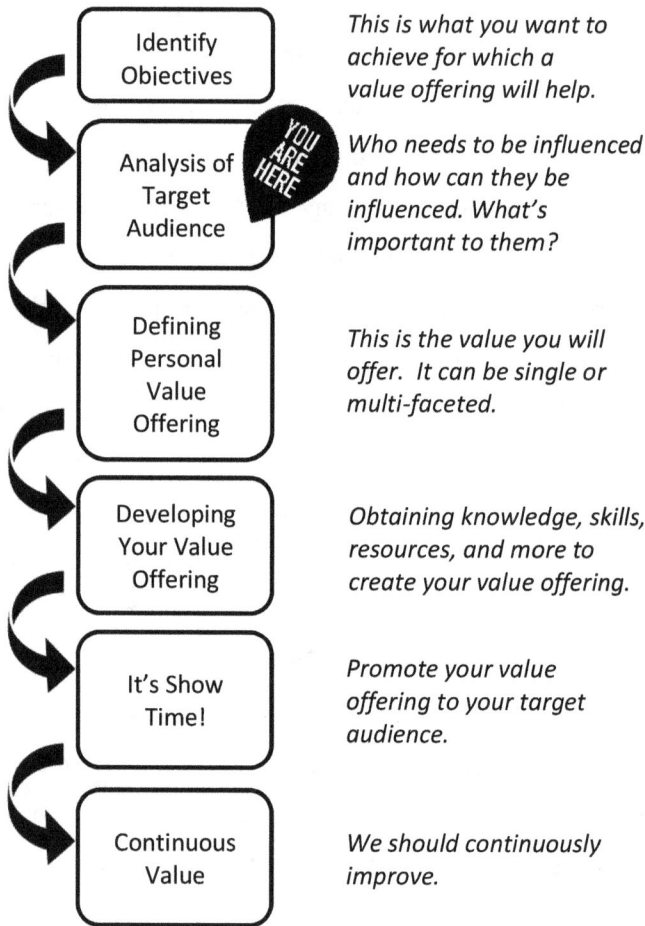

The target audience is that person or persons you intend to influence in your favor. Those persons are the decision makers you want to accept your offer, to hire you for that new job, to benefit from your offer. It may be the family and friends you want to help. It may be the hiring manager or your boss. It may be your current or new prospective customers.

Just telling the childcare center's hiring manager, your target audience, that you are an expert at caring for young children based on years of childcare experience may not be pertinent when the hiring manager is interested in hiring a new team manager. You need to demonstrate supervisory, management, and other skills that will likely influence that hiring manager. That person you are trying to convince to make a decision in your favor is going to be guided by that broader scope – ability to care for young children *and* team leadership. That person has specific requirements for you and she is going to hire you if you have a value offering that is relevant. So, be relevant to your target audience.

But what is that person thinking about when she is listening to you in that interview? How is she evaluating you? Is she being influenced in your favor or against you? What will entice her to agree with you or at least pick you? What is important to her? You could ask these questions during the interview and it is quite fine to do so. However, the interviewer is called an "interviewer" for a reason. *She* is asking *you* the questions. You need to conduct as much research as possible before the interview – know your target audience before your interview.

So, how do we know what may be important to our target audience before we meet them? This is very important and you can do this. Let's start here:

1. Understand your subject matter and be an expert
2. Understand what *you* consider to be important
3. Understand the influencers on your target audience

4. Understand what the decision maker requires for the opportunity you seek

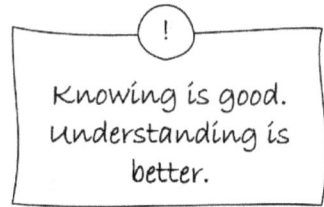

> ! Knowing is good. Understanding is better.

1. Understand your subject matter and be an expert.

Of course, right? The key here is forming an in depth understanding of your subject matter and being able to perform with reliable expertise. You noticed that this does not appear to pertain to "knowing your target audience". Perhaps not directly, but it is quite relevant. Having a highly advanced level of knowledge and expertise in your chosen subject will position you to have tremendous insight into your target audience given they, too, are experienced in the same subject. You also can determine what is important from your perspective and incorporate that into your value offering. Knowing a lot about what your target audience wants does not mean much if you do not know your subject well enough to impress them. *Understand* your profession and be able to reliably perform with the highest of standards.

Being an expert on your subject matter and forming your views of what is important can further help you foresee what other people may consider important. While each of us will differ in our views to some degree, we often share common interests. So, what is important to you may be important to your target audience as well. Then, having this advance level of knowledge and expertise positions you to understand how someone can view a particular facet as important, or not important. Even if you disagree on whether or not some facet is important, your ability to understand how your target audience is thinking helps you foster a productive information-based dialogue.

For example, say you are a physical therapist. With years of education and perhaps a few years of practice, you know the academic information, theory, case study examples, and more. You can define and describe things like ataxia, hyperextension, abduction and adduction, flexion, kyphosis, hypotonic, and spasticity. You can diagnose conditions and form treatment regimens. You know how to use an array of equipment. You are a good physical therapist. But good is not good enough.

Any medical field is complex and dynamic. There is a ton of information to know and there are many changes that come about with new patient cases, research, science, and technology development. It is understandable that no physical therapist knows everything in their field. How much do *you* know, though? Do you proactively research so you are ready for that next case? Do you conduct studies? Do you survey your patients for their inputs? Do you identify and study the use of more equipment, devices, and other tools of the trade? How much do you engage with colleagues to benefit from their experience and lessons learned? Do you pursue leadership roles on committees, in working groups, or on boards where you gain expertise in administration and legal and regulatory influences? Are you truly an expert in diagnosing conditions and at tailoring improved treatments to best serve individual clients?

Beyond the specific discipline of physical therapy, do you have good complimentary skills? Are you empathetic towards patients? Do you communicate well? Do you connect with patients in a way that comforts them and gains their confidence? Are you a good co-worker who contributes to a robust working environment so that everyone benefits?

A desirable value offering by a person in this line of work is so much more than just what is learned in school. One must continuously learn and perfect primary and complimentary skills. This is the beginning of the journey from being a good physical therapist to a great physical therapist, or even to be a great managing physical therapist who guides and mentors others to improve the quality of treatment to all patients. Being a great physical therapist is in the spirit of professional and ethical conduct. With additional knowledge and expertise, you will know much about how people in your profession make their decisions when interviewing you, considering you for a special program or some other opportunity.

The ways by which people learn more or ways by which we hone our skills vary. Consider the following ways as examples:

Classes and other forms of training, preferably ones that provide certifications or degrees. Training is widely available. Many fields of expertise have continuing education requirements and these are often satisfied by completing approved courses. Take more courses than the minimum. There are several providers of courses (not just colleges) and many of them provide certificates that may be recognized in your industry. Maybe it is Wound Management for physical therapists, Certified

Information Security Manager for cyber security professionals, Certified Management Accountant for financial managers, or Society for Human Resource Management Certified Professional for HR professionals.

Study trade material like books, manuals, journals, and other publications. Seems like every industry has a journal or trade association of some type. These are very important to the members of the industry to enhance standards, promote education, and to communicate. With the advent of the internet, there is a wealth of information readily available to us. Please ensure the sources and the information they provide are credible, though.

Consult with colleagues and others who are experts in the subject matter. In my early career years, I worked in the legal field. I spent a lot of time helping with court cases and preparing what seems like thousands of legal documents for many clients. We use to say, "if you ask two lawyers for an opinion on one topic, you'll get three opinions." So...ask around. Everyone has different experiences, varying levels and types of education, and certainly differing perspectives. Our cultural and societal elements also influence the way we think and form opinions. Do not just rely on your own knowledge, nor do not limit yourself to asking only one other person for information. Consult with many. You will likely consider most, if not all, of the information. You may disregard some of it, too. But at least you have an abundance of information on the subject from which to learn and, thereby, enhance your expertise.

Consult with others like an interview. Be specific about what you seek. Inform your colleagues of the reason you are seeking information and that should guide them in providing information that is germane. Ask about their approaches to specific situations and circumstances, their perceived implications of new regulations or standards being implemented, industry and customer trends, approaches to professional development, ideas of innovation (i.e., thoughts on how to make things better), and whatever else comes to mind.

Conduct more practice and have people evaluate you. We are always learning. Even when we may not be interested in learning, we are learning. We learn even more when we are interested in doing so. Be interested in learning. Want to be better and commit to it. The fact that you are reading this book tells me that you are interested in being better at something. That is a good sign, I like it.

Seek out evaluations. Solicit feedback from your peers, bosses, and customers on your work performance, your ideas and opinions, and your decisions. A very effective approach is to practice or demonstrate some job function, like a rehearsal, and ask for an observer's review. If an actual demonstration is not feasible, consider a walk-through or simulation. If you manage a team, you can describe your approach to managing processes and perhaps share your ideas on a way to improve them. Solicit feedback. If you manage databases, you can describe how you audit inputted data for accuracy, manage requests for reports and their production (i.e., customer service), conduct periodic database management functions, and more.

Solicit feedback. So many people are shy to receive their boss' review of their work performance. I have been in management positions for well over 30 years and this was one of the most significant problems I tried to tackle with any of my teams. I get it. When I just started in the adult working world, I felt like the boss would only comment on my performance when I messed up or when he thought I should do better even when I thought I was doing fine. It took me a while, but I eventually realized and accepted how valuable feedback from my bosses, my colleagues, and certainly my customers can be. Never lose out on opportunities to learn from other people.

Research laws, regulations, and other governing resources. Many industries are highly regulated, and for good reason. Rules – I refer to laws and regulations, operating procedures, and similar requirements - can protect consumers and employees alike. Each of us learns about the rules that govern our roles. Take time to learn about the larger inventory of rules that govern your industry, your field of work. Understanding the bigger picture can help us better understand the reasons we have to do the things our bosses are telling us to do. This also helps prepare you for new roles such as supervisory roles.

Take this a step further and keep abreast of current and prospective changes in those rules. Why? Advance notice gives you time to prepare and time to form your input to the team so everyone can be ready. Sounds like a really good value offering there. Imagine the interviewer asking about your thoughts on the upcoming Government regulation on hazardous waste, its labeling, disposal, and reporting, and you were not aware of it. (If you are not involved with hazardous waste, pretend with me.) Why hasn't your current team mentioned this? More importantly, why are you not studying your industry better? When you are selling yourself in that interview or in your request for new roles where you may already work, being able to provide good ideas on how you will apply or work within the new changes is extraordinarily valuable. That's vision. That's proactive teamwork. That's value.

Survey public (i.e., customers) sentiment towards the subject matter. All of us have customers. All of us. Regardless of our profession, there is someone who receives something from each of us. It may be a product or service with a point of sale where there is money involved, which is the most readily recognizable. But there is so much more. The scheduler at an automobile repair shop, in addition to helping customers in a phonecall, provides customer service to the entire shop team. He is collecting information to help assign the right person for the repair job. He is managing workload by not overbooking appointments or by spreading the difficult repair jobs across the team. He is engaging with the caller to ensure they are comfortable with being that paying customer for the shop which means team paychecks. Everyone who receives support from the scheduler is a customer.

Regardless of who your customers are, or who they may be when you are in the position you seek, ask them for their thoughts on the business, the products and services, the customer service and its processes, and more. In customer service positions, our objective is to make customers happy. It is quite difficult to do that without input and feedback from our customers. People vary in their expectations and in what makes them happy. What makes sense to us may not work for a customer. Ask them and learn from their answers.

2. *Understand what you consider to be important.*

This may seem too elementary to discuss here. It is not. Of course you already know what is important. All of us are quick to form opinions and views of many things, to include deciding what we consider important or unimportant. Sometimes it is so easy that we decide what is important within milliseconds of hearing or seeing something. This is also how all of us get ourselves into trouble and oddly we do not learn our lessons very well. Caution caution. Please be diligent.

The field of psychology is full of studies on this topic. Our concern does not need to be over the rapidity by which we make our decisions on what is important to us. It should be more on how we make our decisions. Our interest should be in whether we are applying *intuitive thinking* or *rational thinking* to our decision making. Intuitive thinking is like quick gut-reactions or making decisions based on gut feelings. These can occur very quickly. Rational thinking involves an analysis of information such as the immediate circumstances one is facing and the goals they want to achieve by making a particular decision. It may appear that rational thinking takes more time than intuitive thinking. It certainly can, but it can also happen just as quickly.

For example, when we are well educated and experienced on a subject, whether from academic study or life experiences, we can very quickly apply rational thinking for a quick decision. At some point, many of us are so comfortable with a subject or a situation that we appropriately react very quickly. There is little need for guessing or relying on intuition in this case.

You would be correct in suspecting that I favor rational thinking. I often use the term *fact-based decision making*. When making your decisions, do so based upon a thorough assessment of credible information. Have a good reason for your decisions. In view of the topic of this chapter, I refer to decisions on what is important to you on a particular subject matter. Be ready to answer the question, "why do you believe that?" or "why is that important to you?" If you struggle to form an answer, you may not have based your decision on facts but perhaps on a quick gut feeling. Or worse, it was just a guess in which you really did not believe. When you decide what is important to you, ask yourself the question, "why is this important to me and do I really believe my answer?"

Expand your level of education and expertise on your subject, and you will be able to form more credible decisions on what is and is not important to you. This will contribute directly to the development of your value offering and to a substantive and compelling conversation with your target audience.

3.   Understand the influencers on your target audience.

What makes them tick? What are they considering when making their decisions? What are those influencers? By "influencers" I mean those things that influence a person's decision making behavior.

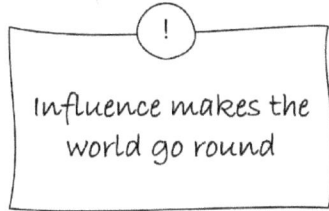

> Influence makes the world go round

You have surely noticed when someone is particularly keen on something. There is something important to them as they consider their decisions. You and I are that way, too. What influences other people may not influence us in the same way, and vice versa. We will also have some common influencers. There are always influencers upon each of us.

I have chaired many interview panels and I was always amazed at the diversity in influencers among the panelists. I could have five panelists helping me with an interview and each one of them seemed to form their questions around one thing that was important to themselves. Sometimes I would rather they broaden their line of questioning, but I understood that each panelist was going to have their own influencers and that is one of the main reasons I would include multiple people in the interviews. Whoever we hired would work with all of us and that candidate needed a good value offering that was appealing to more people on the team than just to me.

Each of us is influenced by many things. How we react to those influencers is formed much by our cultural and societal upbringings and current settings, education (recall the focus we gave this topic earlier), experiences (we discussed this one, too), family teachings, work environments, trends in public opinions and behaviors, and much more. We form values and biases from living in and being exposed to an array of environments.

Twenty-four years of military service instilled a tremendous expectation in me for high standards in respect and teamwork, among other traits. That undoubtedly formed me to favor people who are attentive and courteous to others, and people who value teamwork with no tolerance of leaving anyone behind on a project. One does not need military service to value these particular traits I mention. I am simply stating that for me it was my military service that especially formed me in this way.

Perhaps a work environment may have taught you to give an eager novice a chance rather than always selecting a seasoned expert for a new position – you may recall being that eager novice who was given a chance and now you are rocking the world at what you do. I have fired and reassigned "seasoned professionals" who may have known a lot, but did not work hard or could not play well with others. I have hired novices who were motivated and interested in learning more and showed they would be valuable contributions to the team. Many different settings, many different influences.

Look around at the people in your work place, your family, or your friends. Do you know someone who is always asking questions because they like information – an Information Hound? An English major who is a stickler for composition, syntax, and spelling and loves to edit your documents? Someone who shows more interest in the next step than the current step – the one who says "OK, *but then what?*". Someone who often talks about sports like they watch every game and studies every statistic? How about someone who is always talking about deadlines and not much more than that? They each have something that influences them and in turn it influences others.

That variety of influencers includes you and me. Just like all those other people have a favored interest, you and I have varying interests driven by influencers on our decision making. While I am pointing out that influencers can vary, let us recognize that many of us will have common influencers as well. Most of us will be attracted to politeness and courtesy over bad attitudes and ill manners, and we may be attracted to one's knowledge of the subject matter and potential to perform well. So, as we proceed we will consider our own influencers in addition to our target audience's influencers we hope to identify.

Let's start with you. If you were on the receiving end of a person's presentation of their value offering, what would be important to you? Your first answer at this moment should be, "It depends on the topic or situation." Are we talking about a job interview for my team or the kid next door who wants to cut my grass? Got it. Let us go with the job interview for a position on your team. You may be the hiring manager. If you are not the hiring manager, envision being a panelist at the interview who will ask questions of the candidates and then cast recommendations to the hiring manager. (I have been the hiring manager for so many positions I can't recall all of them. I always included interview panelists who would be peers to the candidate we hire. I saw that as my value offering to my organizations for team building and optimization of performance and work culture.)

Let us say you work for a company that provides outsourcing services for billing management. Your company's clients, or customers, are other companies who use you to manage their billing. This includes receiving payments from your customers' customers, managing their billing accounts, preparing interim and end-of-year reporting, and providing on-call and online resources.

What would be important to you to see in the candidate's value offering? You may be interested in a candidate's reliability in being very thorough and accurate with numerical figures and reporting, and this is especially important to you because your team's accuracy in its reporting has been declining over the past year. The candidate may be flexible in work schedules or even preferring to work night shifts – your company operates 15-hours a day 7 days a week because your clients are located across the country in different time zones. The candidate may be highly capable of operating your Customer Relations Management/Billing system and knows many tricks to help your team use it more effectively and efficiently. You may be, and I suggest you ought to be, considering things like demeanor, attitude, language, and other such complimentary traits that can contribute to or degrade a positive work culture and teamwork.

Consider everything you identified as important to you as the interviewer and reverse roles. You are now the candidate and you are the one who needs to present *your* value offering. You are seeking a new position on the team or somewhere else in the company or with another company in the same line of work. You have some understanding, maybe a lot of understanding, of the influencers on your interviewer's decision making behavior. This understanding goes a long way to forming your value offering. This is more than just forming answers to say in the interview to get the job. This is the forming of your value offering that is intended to last a long time during your new role.

Add more insight. Ask for input. You identified what influences you, those things that are important to you. Now ask about influencers your colleagues, friends, and other people have. Are they influenced by a person's attention to detail? Good personal chemistry? College degree? A specific type of experience? Communication skills? Adeptness with information systems? Certifications? Coffee making skills? What would they want out of a candidate's value offering?

Take that line of questioning a step further. Try to get them to explain why their influencers are important. Ensure they provide rational answers. Recall *rational thinking*? All that education and work experience you obtained will help you in assessing and understanding their rational. This can help you significantly in deciding which of their influencers you may consider in eventually forming your value offering.

There can be far too many influencers to consider when forming your value offering. Some influencers will conflict with each other in that they are not compatible. Some may not even be relevant. This is like identifying everything in the grocery store, then picking what you want to put in your cart. Do not, though, readily exclude influencers just because you may not like them. You may have encountered an opportunity to learn from those other people. By understanding their reasons behind their influencers, you may discover that they are important. You may discover that a lot of people have the same influencers and your value offering may need to consider them.

Here is a case example of the point I am trying to make in the preceding paragraph. I once managed an executive team responsible for supporting a large Government organization of about 1700 people. My team at that time consisted of 16 staff personnel. All were very senior with many years of experience. Great people, I really liked each of them a lot. There was a bit of lethargy in some, though. Some people were set in their ways and got "comfy" by just riding out the days. I will not go as far as saying they were consciously deciding on a poor work performance. I was informed by my hiring manager that they were not adequately motivated nor held accountable by my predecessor. As a result, they worked to the level their previous boss condoned. Shortly after I was hired to manage the team, I started hearing from customers, some of them senior managers of other offices, that the team was not as helpful as they needed to be.

My evaluation of the situation identified two conditions I wanted to fix: Lack of fresh expertise and a marginally motivated work environment. I hired a couple more people at mid-level positions who brought fresh expertise and views to our line of work. They injected much needed energy to the team and provided new ideas on staff processes and standards. That was the easy part. The tough one was adding an office manager position to the team and hiring a young inexperienced person who just graduated from college. People around me wanted me to hire another senior expert so the workload could be spread out more. I did not see that they had too much work on their plates, just that they were not working effectively enough. My influencers at this point were a desire for positive office environments and livelier teams. This already existed to some degree among a few staff members, but I was determined to turn it up a notch. Many people on my staff were highly motivated and the work environment was generally positive, yet it was not as consistent nor widespread as I wanted. This was not a problem caused by the team, it was the result of people being so inwardly focused and busy that they did not have much time to interact in a way to energize each other. This was a work condition condoned by the previous boss over a few years.

I wanted to add an office manager (executive assistant) to help with our communications, processing of paperwork and task management, and a number of other office process functions to free the rest of the team to engage one another better. That would include them engaging with customers more often and more readily. I was also looking for a lessening of the stress across the team caused by, mostly their misconception, that there was too much work to do and their customers were unpleasant people. The tail was wagging the dog big time here.

I hired a young lady just graduating from college who was young enough to be our daughter or even our granddaughter. She had no experience in our line of work. But, but, she was smart. She impressed me with her thoughts on office organization, surprisingly. She was personable. She was motivated. Chemistry was spot-on. People adored her. She demonstrated a keen ability to perform the role I wanted her to fill. After I hired her, I had to fight off other office leads who wanted to hire her away from me. She jumped right in and took charge of our processes and our communications like a seasoned expert, and most importantly instilled a vibrant work environment. There was a new found positive energy across the team. Compliments from our customers on the team's improved performance vis a vis positive, responsive, and attentive behavior was a reliably consistent occurrence. This started with my influencer – a long work history rooted in high standards of motivated teamwork - and was delivered by our new office manager. If you were to ask me for my reason this influencer was important to me, the above is my answer. Knowing this may or may not compel you to consider this important to your value offering some day, but knowing it allows you to make that decision.

So far we have been collecting information close by us from the easy sources: You and the people around you. Yet this insight is still important because much, if not all of it, will be relevant. That assumes to some degree that your current line of work, or whatever your setting, is akin to what you are seeking with your newly developing value offering. Those people who you hope to impress with your value offering may have similar influencers. We will now focus on identifying the influencers of our target audience. This can be more challenging, yet it is achievable. And, it is important.

The first thing to consider is your own education and experience on the subject. Yes, I am going there again. *Any journey to there starts where we are here.* In fact, much of what you will read here in a moment may have been part of your education and your experience.

Then, I recommend reviewing media coverage and other public commentary such as customer reviews. Any organization worth joining is one that takes public feedback seriously. As such, people and their decision making will be influenced by that feedback. You should know what that feedback is. Sometimes the information you find will pertain to an industry, a market, or some other broader audience and not the specific company or organization. This is still valuable in that a specific organization (e.g., a company or Government office or a non-profit organization) where you intend to meet that decision maker should be knowledgeable and interested in that same information.

Here is a sample of sources to research. Nowadays, information is widely published for access via the internet. There is a plethora of credible sources there.

➢ *News media.* Look for objective reporting. There is a lot of biased coverage nowadays on just about any topic. Look past that. There are many news media sources that focus on business and consumer affairs.

➤ *"Watchdog" and consumer groups.* Many industries, companies, and even non-profit organizations are closely monitored and reported upon by these groups.

➤ *Government reporting.* Much Government reporting provides statistics and forecasts. From this data you can identify trends, potential Government regulatory actions, and industry forecasts. Research federal, state, and local (city, county) sources.

➤ *Customer reviews.* These can be viewed on a company's website, from a variety of customer review service providers, and from social media sources. Consider reviews of the companies themselves as well as their products and services. As the cliché goes – I take these with a grain of salt. What one person adores another person detests. Nonetheless, we can gain insight into what customers of your target audience are saying and you may have a desirable value offering that can increase the ratio of *adores* to *detests* for your target audience.

➤ *Journals and other scholarly resources.* From these sources we can obtain information on a wide variety of subjects. We can research fields of medicine, engineering, law, management, sciences, and much more that may be relevant to our target audience. Our target audience may actively use these sources as well, and even contribute to their published content.

One of the most important forms of information for me pertains to that which governs my target audience. I am referring to laws, regulations, policies, and the like. For most of my working life I worked in fields and for organizations that were highly regulated. To survive and to perform well I quickly grew to appreciate and to know what governed me. It is one of my many influencers.

Laws and regulations (I will use these terms to roughly include all governances) are implemented for numerous reasons such as public health and safety, fairness to consumers, and funding of Government purses, to name a few. All of us are expected to comply, yet many of us are not fully aware of everything that governs us. There is a lot there, so it is understandable that many of us do not know all of it. And the rules change and it can be difficult to keep up with them. We do need to try, though. And people in management positions are expected to stay on top of this, provide the education, and enforce the rules. Part of our value offering must be to do this and to do this well. Also, those managers may be the hiring manager at our interview and we need to know much of what they know.

Imagine you are an electrician or working in the construction industry where electricians are involved and you were not aware of the latest changes to the National Electrical Code. "So, Steve, we are nearly complete renovating multiple houses for our clients and the latest NEC changes require us to move a bunch of outlets and replace some with GCFI outlets. That is going to require us to pull new permits and we do not know how to meet our deadlines. How do you think we should approach this?"

Spoiler alert - "Uhhh, there was a change?" won't cut it. Not even a sincere shoulder shrug.

Imagine seeking a position with a company where you would manage its intellectual property. This would be managing trademarks and copyrights and patents with Government registrations and oversight in its use in the company's marketing operations. You have not done your homework to know that rules changed in how to renew trademarks. A competitor is now using your company's intellectual material for their business gain and you cannot do anything about it. Oops.

Researching laws and regulations can be daunting. I really like to research and even I am easily overwhelmed with this. It should be done though. Do not fret over it. Be smart on it. Here is a list of some of the sources to use:

1.   Industry trade journals
2.   Government publications.   There   are   many   Government publications on a variety of topics. Some are topic-specific and are published as pamphlets and similar easy-to-use formats. For the adventurous, there are the law books, Code of Federal Regulations, and Internal Revenue Code to name only a few.
3.   Union publications
4.   Company policy statements
5.   Municipal zoning codes, building codes, and other regulations
6.   Industry professional organizations. Most industries have them.

7. Nonprofit Organizations. Many NPOs actively engage Government offices to influence legislation and regulation. Some, like watchdog groups, operate to monitor and report on violations of laws and regulations.

Next, let's zero in on the specific target. What your research has thus far uncovered can be invaluable. Now add to it some target-specific information. This is information directly about the specific organization, a specific team within that organization, or the specific decision makers you want to influence. This can be the most difficult to collect and, honestly, it can be impossible. However, there are opportunities and they will only produce results when you try.

We now try to learn more about a manager of a team we want to join. We learned about a particular organization. We are now at the decision maker level of our research. I am not advocating anything illegal or unethical. No wire tapping or espionage, no breaking into the office. Don't go there. I am talking about collecting publicly available information.

Here is a good start:

➤ *Social media profiles*. Many people have professional profiles on social media sites in which they describe their roles and post information about their work views. They often list their work history and you can gain insight into their experience from that information. Many will connect with other people and organizations which provides you insight into their personal interests. Look for those who may be managers or even prospective co-workers and learn about them. Many organizations have social media sites where someone in a public affairs role speaks about the organization. I use these sites and it is amazing how much information is there.

> *Organization literature and other forms of advertising.* Review what the organization is saying about itself. You will learn about its mission or purpose for existing, its products and services, corporate social responsibility program, working code of conduct, new operations, hiring trends, and much more. Attend trade shows and conferences where your target organization is promoting itself.

> *Financial status.* This can be important for someone seeking a corporate growth position, Chief Financial Officer position, or a similar position responsible for the financial status of a company. Some reporting is publicly available. For publicly traded companies, a review of their stock or other publicly traded information can be quite useful. Researching information published by the business-focused media can be valuable.

> *Observe On The Ground.* Visit as a customer and buy something. Collect literature and talk with the staff to learn more. This also can help you decide whether or not you may be interested in a position there. Observe operations and customer behavior. Form

thoughts on how you can improve upon what you observe. I have met some very detailed people who would observe office décor and desk décor and tchotchkes looking for topics of conversation for a personal-level connection. Seeing a baseball pennant, they would strike up a conversation about baseball. A family picture at the beach, they talk about their family's last vacation to the beach. Look for these items as you report for your interview.

Add more to these tactics I present. Please consider the tactics I introduce only as a start. Additional ones should be identified to best suit the situations and circumstances you face.

I am going to walk through another scenario with additional detail to help demonstrate this phase. In this scenario we want to improve training at our company. Nearly everyone I meet believes training can be greatly improved where they work. And they are right. I have worked at many places and with many teams. I have also been a consultant helping organizations with training – setting up training teams and programs, curriculum development, teaching. I have never found one place that had a training program that did not need improvement. Some had good components, most had good people trying to make it work. Yet for a variety of reasons, none were optimal. I far too often witness people and teams fail because of a lack of good training, or no training at all. I suspect most of you have similar experiences, so this ought to be a good subject to use for this scenario.

You want to see improvements in your company's training program. You will offer to the Training Director to serve in a role on the training team. You are not certain whether that will be full-time or part-time yet. How will you convince her that she needs someone to help? How will you convince her that someone is you? You will present to her your winning value offering in a way that appeases her interests that her influencers created. We need to better understand how she would make her decision and that understanding develops from our knowledge and understanding of her influencers and resulting interests.

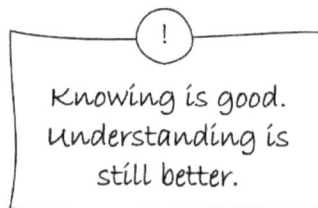

> Knowing is good. Understanding is still better.

Recall, in this phase we are identifying influencers and the interests our target audiences have that form their decision making behavior. We are not forming our value offering or deciding on what we intend to do to improve the training program at this point. That comes later. Right now we are looking for those influencers, those things that guide the Training Director's interests in her decision making.

What Are The Influencers On You?

I like to start here for two reasons. First, what influences you may also influence others. This can be a good start in identifying potential influencers in your target audience. People may be different from each other, but we are at times surprisingly similar to each other. Secondly, your influencers will certainly guide you in forming your eventual value offering. Knowing the influencers upon you and your target audience will help you fine-tune your value offering and frame how you present your value offering, and yourself, to your target audience.

I am going to list a few ideas of influencers below, yet take time to identify your influencers before reading my list. Think of what influences you on the subject of company training.

The following influences my decision making on the subject of training programs:

> *I want relevant training (i.e., it supports the current and future needs of the employees).* Experts in training program and curriculum development incorporate Needs Assessments. A Needs Assessment identifies needs across the organization for knowledge, skills, types of accessibility to training, and more. In order for training to be valuable, it needs to be relevant and timely. Relevant means it must provide the knowledge a person needs to perform their job well. It must enable the development of skills for the person to perform their job well. It must be refreshed so that it meets current needs. It must be provided in a way that employees can access it such as via online tools either live or prerecorded, video or classroom instruction, reading materials, etc. A consistent failing of training programs, as I have seen, has been a lack of relevancy where training materials were developed by trainers who decided on their own what was relevant, although with good intentions, vice thoroughly assessing needs with input from the workforce and their managers. And I have seen training

provided only after a significant deficiency in a team's work performance is noted. The training is still important, but it is late. Timely training can and should mitigate the risk of performance deficiency.

➢ *My experience with successful delivery methods.* Forming training content for a presentation is very important, yet it means nothing if it cannot be effectively delivered to and understood by students. Some people may learn better by watching a video than reading a book, or with hands-on training more than a lecture. Sometimes the topic itself warrants a specific delivery model. For example, reading a pamphlet on the requirements for labeling warehouse supplies may suffice. Reading a pamphlet for how to operate the forklift may not be as effective as hands-on training by sitting behind the wheel of that forklift. Also, some people may not have the same means of access as others. Some may have ready access to a computer all day and are able to watch a video while others may have a job that does not use a computer and they would need a different form of training delivery. A Needs Assessment can help identify delivery method requirements.

➢ *I want a training team comprised of experts who are committed to providing top quality training.* Expertise is requisite for any good training program. That includes expertise in the training subject matter, expertise in delivery, expertise in training program management (i.e., expertise in assessing needs, evaluating the program, administration, instruction, engaging company leadership for support and resources, etc). Occasionally I accept that training program staff may not need to be subject matter experts in workforce job-specific subjects. There can be so many subjects that it can be impractical to staff a training team with experts in all subjects. However, subject matter experts should contribute to the preparation of training materials and perhaps in the presentation of the training. Those experts can come from the company's own workforce or temporary hires and consultants.

So much more is required than just handing out booklets or writing on a board in a classroom, or spam emailing people about training deadlines. You with me? The training team must expertly assess training needs, develop curriculum and materials, manage resources, evaluate program effectiveness, and maintain ongoing support from organization leadership for resources and enforcement, and perhaps even more.

➢ *My experience with a lack of company leadership support that led to training program failures.* Company leadership must support training. It is that simple. The company needs to hire experts to manage their training programs, timely provide sufficient resources, and advocate and enforce training expectations.

➢ *Accommodation needs.* This is an extension of my comments regarding delivery methods. I am influenced a lot by the diversity in the people around me, and in a good way. I recognize that people differ in the way they learn and in the way they are able to access training. Additionally, some people with disabilities may need specialized systems or facility access. There really is no one-size-fits-all approach to training. Training is for the benefit of whom? The student, right? Training needs to cater to the student.

What influencers did you identify? Your list may be very different than mine and that is fine. We may share some of these influencers. Here are some additional influencers we may consider:

- Requirements for licenses and certifications
- Professional association standards. There are professional associations within many industries to promote standards in education, certifications, ethics, and more.
- Health and safety interests. The training program may include physical training, or training on topics of health and safety.
- Laws and regulations
- Geographical displacement of the workforce
- Languages and cultural differences of the workforce
- Security and sensitivity of the information and of company operations
- Upcoming changes in the organization
- Business competition

On the following page is a form you can use for an individual or group exercise. Identify a scenario around your objective: Seeking a specific job or opportunity, for example. For groups, conduct a brain storming session using this format on dry erase boards or easel pads. Identify a number of scenarios and solicit unjudged input from everyone. Identify influencers to a target audience decision making and explain reasons they are important to consider. Notice the diversity of inputs and the value in understanding them.

Influencers (on me or target audience)	Reason These Influencers Are Important For Me To Understand

- Ponder Page -

Chapter 4

Define Your
Value Offering

We conducted a lot of homework and now it is time to start defining our value offering. Exciting!

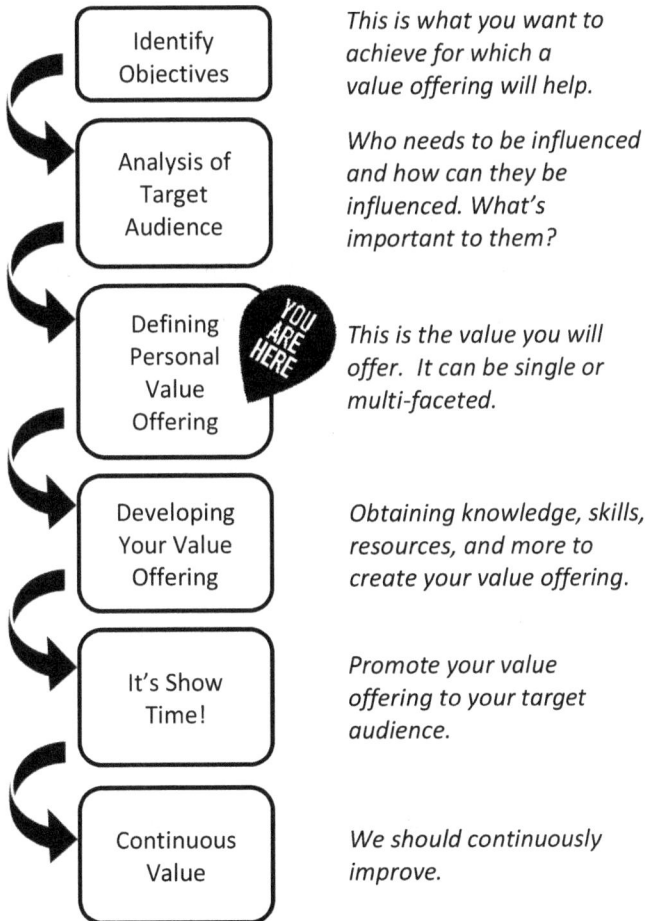

Step	Description
Identify Objectives	*This is what you want to achieve for which a value offering will help.*
Analysis of Target Audience	*Who needs to be influenced and how can they be influenced. What's important to them?*
Defining Personal Value Offering **YOU ARE HERE**	*This is the value you will offer. It can be single or multi-faceted.*
Developing Your Value Offering	*Obtaining knowledge, skills, resources, and more to create your value offering.*
It's Show Time!	*Promote your value offering to your target audience.*
Continuous Value	*We should continuously improve.*

What does it mean to define our value offering? By "define" I mean we will craft and describe our value offering. It is not creating or forming a value offering. You have already done much of that through the decisions you have made during your life based on your experiences, education, guidance from others, and multiple other sources. You will continue developing it in the same way, and hopefully in a way that continuously improves it. We will be discussing that in the next chapter.

Crafting will include the wording or writing of your value offering as it may currently stand or as you intend to further develop it to be. *Describing* brings in explanatory details to help people understand your value offering. I tend to prefer using a single sentence in *crafting* a value offering – it is like a value offering statement. The description of your value offering provides the substance of what it entails. More on this in a moment.

There are three criteria of a value offering I would like you to consider. These are:

1. Relevancy
2. Realism
3. Understandability

Be Relevant. Being relevant is a way of ensuring your offering is actually valuable. Your value offering with your supporting expertise, abilities, intentions, demeanor, etc., must satisfy your target audience's wants and needs.

For example, say you are a loan officer helping customers with home loans. Your value offering may be to provide guidance that is timely, easy-to-understand, and comprehensive to all customers that leads to identifying several loan options and guides your customers to making the right borrowing decisions. You do this by being an expert on, and providing expertise on, all loan programs offered by your financial institution. You include your ability to rationally recommend the best loan program for the customer's specific circumstances and goals. You ensure you are current on all loan requirements and loan options so your customers receive the latest information. You perform as an advocate for your customers to get their loan application approved through the underwriting process and not just being a loan salesperson who treats all customers as only a numbered caller.

You are very timely with your communications and in accomplishing the loan process milestones to ensure you and your customers meet all of the home sales contract deadline requirements. This latter topic means you are also knowledgeable of the home buying process. There are other components that can apply depending on what your customers - your target audience - want from you. If you do all of this, you are relevant to your target audience. If you miss any of this, you may not be considered relevant. When we are not relevant, we lose out and the people relying on us can lose, too.

In crafting a value offering that is relevant, consider the interests of your target audience and your own interests. By now you would have gathered a good amount of information to help you understand these. This goes a long way to being relevant. By considering your target audience's interests you craft an offering that is valuable in their eyes. Keep in mind that you are selling yourself to someone (figuratively…), so you need to be relevant in view of the interests of those other people. We have also identified our own interests. This is exceptionally important in that you are the expert in what you do and, as such, you can also offer value that your target audience may not have considered. This is good team work.

Be Real. Your value offering must also be real. Not just sound real, but actually be real. In other words, you are able to do all the things you need to do in order to deliver on your value offering. If your value offering is to guarantee your software company's call center will resolve all trouble calls for software support in terms of each callers' needs, your value offering is not realistic. There will be customers with needs we cannot accommodate. Some of the callers' needs may be unrealistic. Some may require support beyond our level of ability. The word "guarantee" is the stumbling block here.

Using another example, if your value offering is to timely develop and implement sustainable process improvements for the business operations of your client's company, that could be realistic. Its realism would rely upon your ability to deliver and that ability may include expertise in Business Process Engineering/Re-engineering, operations analysis, organization development, and other relevant disciplines. Oh, there's that "relevant" word again.

There is no value in a promise if you cannot deliver on that promise. Having the ability to deliver on your value offering is essential to your value offering being real. It would also help you if you have a history of being highly successful at delivering on your value offering for other customers. That history of success can lead people to accepting your offering as real on the assumption that you can deliver on your value offering again because you have done it previously.

Be understood. Your value offering must also be understandable. Granted, you can deliver on your value offering even when people do not understand it. However, the education I am trying to impart upon you is in helping you present a value offering that will influence people to make decisions in your favor (i.e., to accept your value offering). This means your target audience should understand your value offering because decisions should be made on information that is understood. Craft and describe your value offering using words, concepts, messages, etc., that are understandable by your target audience.

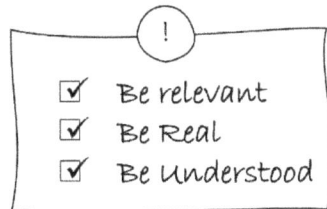

> ☑ Be relevant
> ☑ Be Real
> ☑ Be Understood

On the topic of communications we are taught to "write to our audience". This pertains to verbal communications as well. The point with that guidance is to understand that our audience may not understand our topic to the extent that we understand it. Understand? Use words and terms that are commonly known rather than a vernacular that may be highly specialized or unique to your little world. Get straight to the point and avoid superfluous information and chit chat. Present your messages and supporting information in a logical order. Stay on a message until your audience understands, then move on to the next message.

Let's craft and define some value offering examples and see what these can look like. I like to craft a value offering statement consisting of one or two sentences (usually just one) and then describe it with whatever amount of narrative that is needed to adequately describe it. The value offering statements will be simple yet should be substantive. The descriptions need to explain what you mean by your value offering, such as referring to your skills, education, experience, methods and approaches, etc. These must, of course, be germane to your value offering. Each situation is different, so value offerings and their descriptions will vary widely. Even for multiple people seeking the same opportunity, such as that same job or position on a sports team, each of them may have a different value offering and associated descriptions. I am going to provide a few examples. As you read these, think of ways you would reword your own value offering and how you would describe that value offering differently.

Example 1: (Logistics Program Manager) I reliably deliver success to logistics programs by ensuring timely completion of milestones, superior team performance, program accountability, operating within budget, and a high-level of customer satisfaction.

Description:

* I optimize program operations by providing expertise in all facets of program management and applying a tailored approach focusing on each program's specific requirements.

* I maintain a Project Management Professional certification.

* I provide expertise in developing and applying program management artifacts (e.g., program management plans, risk management plans, quality assurance and quality control plans, master schedules, periodic performance review reports, configuration management plans, and more).

* I tailor program management requirements for a right-fit for each program.

* I am experienced and highly capable of managing changes in program requirements and scope of work.

* I provide team leadership ensuring superior team wide performance, professional development, and high employee retention.

* I am capable at building teams through hiring and transfers, and managing team growth to accommodate long-term program growth or short-term surges.

* I have 15 years of experience working in the logistics industry with a series of roles with progressively increased scope of work and leadership responsibilities.

Example 2: (Advertising Professional) I reliably develop and administer advertising campaigns to obtain profitable customers for significant corporate growth.

Description:

* I provide expertise in market (i.e., customers) analysis to identify markets with desirable revenue and profit potential.

* I develop and administer highly effective advertising campaigns by thoroughly analyzing markets, forming campaign plans, incorporating in-depth knowledge of products and services, fostering company-wide involvement, leveraging a large and tailored portfolio of advertising methods and venues, and continuously monitoring and assessing campaign plan effectiveness.

* I am highly experienced and knowledgeable of advertising strategies, analyzing customer behaviors, and crafting advertising messages.

* I am experienced with and highly capable in event planning for conferences, trade shows, and other advertising events.

* I continuously enhance my expertise, already rooted with college education and 10 years of work experience, with continuing education and with participation in advertising industry professional organizations.

Example 3: (Wedding Planner) I provide you with a memorable wedding, a special celebration of your new beginning and one to treasure forever.

Description:

* I provide an artistic style to all aspects to include the meal, venue, décor, invitations, photography, and entertainment to ensure everyone will enjoy every moment.

* I have a large network of service providers and I will provide my expertise in coordinating their support so you do not have to. I save you time and money.

* I embrace the personal and emotional value of your special event so that your interests are met.

* I tailor the planning to accommodate your budget and personal interests.

* I coordinate with you on all aspects to ensure they satisfy your expectations.

OK, your turn. We will start by defining a value offering for your current position whether it be your current job, your business, a position on a sports team or on a town committee, a new project, whatever. In doing so, we can assess whether our current value offering suffices or there is something we can do better.

When I managed teams, I would have each employee define their value offering. I would do that as soon as I took on my new position as their team manager. Then, sometime in the future I would have them do it again. This was a highly valuable drill that helped people assess themselves and identify ways to improve where it may be needed. It was also extraordinarily helpful to me because the resulting dialogue across the team gave me new ideas – well, actually, most of the ideas were presented by my team during these value offering assessment activities and it was very nice to say "Great idea! Let's do it!" This drill was also valuable as a confidence booster when we recognized how good many value offerings were as is.

As we have studied thus far, consider your own interests for the role you have, the interests you know your bosses and perhaps the organization writ large have, and your capabilities. Consider the requirements placed upon the work you do, upcoming changes, and other influences upon your role. Craft your value offering to be relevant, real, and understandable. Do not craft it as a job description. Craft it to portray what you want to offer that is valuable and the benefit that your value offering will provide. Also, do not be so quick as to craft it to portray what you are currently doing or offering. Remember, this is self-assessment time. Write your ideal value offering. If you are already delivering on it, great! It is infrequent that I meet someone who is, though. So do not be afraid to learn that there is room for improvement. Learning this makes us valuable team members because we are taking steps to perform better for our team. After you crafted your value offering, describe it by noting the multiple ways you will deliver the "things" you will do and your abilities. Grab a pen and paper, a marker and erase board, or chalk and the sidewalk and start writing.

This is the sequence:

First, what is your role?
Second, craft your value offering (1 to 2 sentences).
Third, describe your value offering.

The form on the following page will help you organize your information.

Current or Pursued Role/Position	
Value Offering	
Description	

Have someone review what you wrote. Ask for their honest and objective feedback on the value offering you chose for yourself in relation to your current role. Bosses, get input from those who work for you. Everyone, get input from your peers and bosses. See if they have any additional ideas on what you may include in your description. It's teamwork time!

If you are seeking a new opportunity, conduct this exercise next for that opportunity. What you have learned thus far will help you in preparing for that new opportunity.

For group sessions, have attendees participate together on crafting and describing value offerings. Identify some positions to set the stage and have fun. This approach can yield a great deal of insight and valuable contributions.

- Ponder Page -

Chapter 5

Developing Your
Value Offering

Can you really do it? The answer is "yes!". You are telling people you will be valuable to them. You are pledging value. You are making promises. You must be able to deliver. And how do you do that?

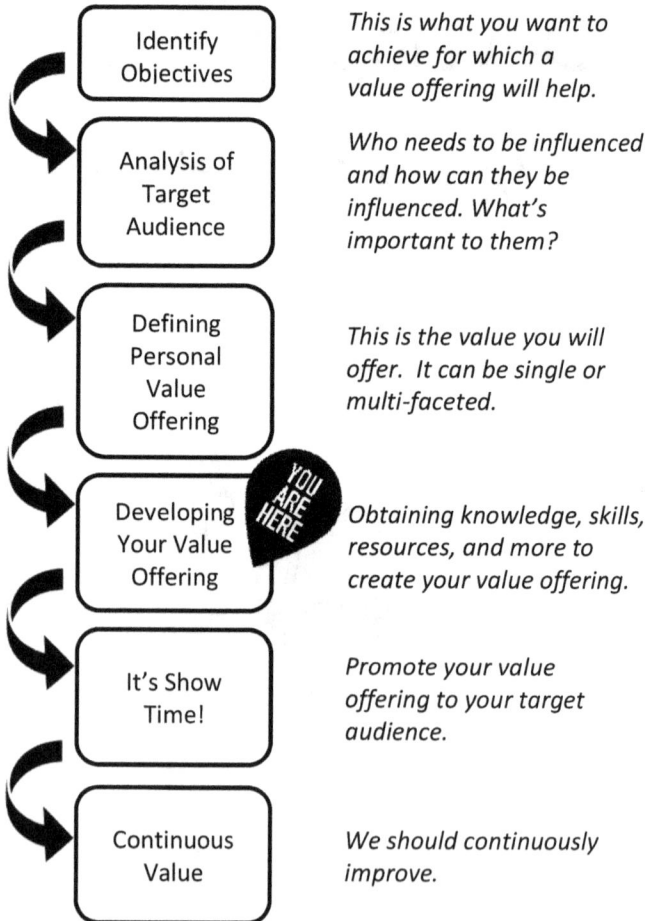

Identify Objectives	*This is what you want to achieve for which a value offering will help.*
Analysis of Target Audience	*Who needs to be influenced and how can they be influenced. What's important to them?*
Defining Personal Value Offering	*This is the value you will offer. It can be single or multi-faceted.*
Developing Your Value Offering YOU ARE HERE	*Obtaining knowledge, skills, resources, and more to create your value offering.*
It's Show Time!	*Promote your value offering to your target audience.*
Continuous Value	*We should continuously improve.*

You defined your value offering, whether for your current position or one you are seeking. For the most part you likely are able to deliver on most of your value offering. We now improve our ability to perform and this is not a one-time episode. Improving ourselves should be a continuous effort. In the spirit of continuous improvement, there is continuous learning. I do not suggest that we should not be confident or satisfied with ourselves today. We certainly should have a positive outlook. Each of you have some tremendous value to provide. My intent is to instill an understanding that no matter how good we are, there are opportunities to do more and to do something better if we so choose. The world around us changes and we may need to change in order to successfully compete.

Our ability to deliver on our value offering requires expert knowledge, skills to implement our knowledge, resources, complimentary traits, and opportunity. We do not get to pick and choose here. Each of these is essential.

The specifics of the above list of requirements are tailored to each situation. The circumstances for each situation will be diverse and, consequently, value offerings and the requirements for delivering those value offerings will likewise be diverse. You will be able to identify your requirements and develop your abilities with the knowledge you already have, additional education, and input from other people. I am going to generally describe these requirements here since the details applicable to you will eventually be determined by you based on the circumstances you face.

Expert knowledge. I break this down into two types: (1) academic and (2) practical. Academic knowledge is what some of us may refer to as *book learning.* The term *theoretical learning* is also often used. Information gained from a book, a class, or a lecture is academic knowledge. This is how we learn about rules, definitions, processes, and so much more that is absolutely critical to understanding a particular subject. If you are seeking a coaching position for the soccer team, you need to know the rules of the game, strategy and goal-scoring plays, the abilities of each of your team's players, the abilities of players on the competing teams, and your practice and game schedules. You gain this academic knowledge from reading, talking with people, thinking and creating plays on paper.

Practical knowledge is gained through practice or hands-on learning. Playing soccer for several years, closely observing your players on the field, and teaching those

> **!**
> Know what to do and have the ability to do it.

goal-scoring plays on the field is practical learning from which you gain practical knowledge. Having the academic knowledge is very important to knowing what you need to do. Practical knowledge forms your ability to do it.

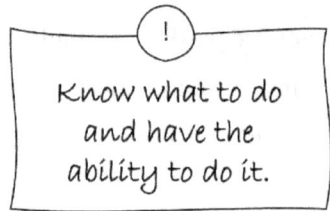

Identify resources for knowledge and practice what you learn. Read the books, take classes, ask colleagues and bosses for information. Refer to Chapter 3 of this book where we discussed multiple forms of information that can be valuable to your research. Incorporate your expert-level academic learning into practice. This is where you develop your skills to deliver your value offering. Do it on the job or on the field or in the kitchen. Practice, practice, practice. While you are practicing, you may discover that you need more academic knowledge. You get that additional knowledge and then you put it into practice. The cycle continues towards continuous improvement.

In this soccer coach scenario, where do we get the academic information we need? Start by identifying the information we need. We need to know the rules, so we read the official Fédération Internationale de Football Association rules. We need to know how to help players improve their speed, agility, kicking accuracy and distance, and endurance. So, we study principles of physical training, physics of body movements, and nutrition. Identify sources of relevant information for your situation and study to learn. Do not just read. Study!

Your practical learning should be applicable to the skills you identify as necessary for your value offering. That means start by identifying the skills you need. A soccer coach should be highly skilled at motivating players, gaining their confidence and attention, creating effective plays, assigning players to positions for which they are best suited, teaching body positions and movements for kicks and steals, and reading the competing team's plays. Skills like these can only come from hands-on practical learning. Practice, practice, practice.

While you are developing your primary skills as they are required for your position, do not forget about complimentary skills. A primary skill for an insurance salesperson may be knowledge of insurance policies and ways to tailor them for customers. A complimentary skill would be good communications or demeanor with customers. Complimentary skills are often overlooked. Sadly, this is true. I see it a lot. It does no good to know how to craft winning soccer plays and explain them to the players if that coach is not good at communicating, motivating people, and following through to help players achieve their maximum potential. Did you ever work for someone who may have known a lot about their job and could complete their tasks to make their own bosses happy, but they did not do a good job at getting along with their own team members? Come on, say it.

Although unacceptable, that situation is understandable. It is easy for us to focus on primary skills and forget about or take for granted important complimentary skills. This is my reason for including this issue in this book. I know many people who start a business with a mindset that they are good at and only need to know a set of primary skills like selling information technology, providing team coaching, or managing programs and they fail to recognize that they also need to communicate well, advertise, have a good image and brand, manage their company's finances, understand laws and regulations pertaining to their business, and much more.

For our sales position we consider the importance of having in-depth knowledge of our company's products, our pricing menu, and how to process the sales transaction. In order to increase the odds of convincing someone to buy our products and to return as a repeat customer, we need some complimentary skills, too.   These include communicating in differing ways to appeal to differing types of people, good body language and personal presentation, an ability to understand our prospective customers, and creativity in forming solutions to meet their needs, and much more.

We need primary skills which are those that pertain to core job functions, yet we also need complimentary skills to round ourselves out. Both are essential.

Here is a small sample list of complimentary skills. In some cases, some of these and others you identify can also be primary skills.

Complimentary Skills

Listening	Kindness
Communications	Selflessness
Proper Speech and Writing	Empathy
Pleasant Demeanor	Studious
Creativity	Visionary
Analytical Ability	Resourceful
Attentiveness	Team Facilitation
Motivated	Problem Solving
Teamwork	Detailed
Organized	Coffee and Cookie Making

We still need that opportunity, though. What good is it to have all this knowledge and these skills without an opportunity to demonstrate them? This is sort of a trick question. Having expert knowledge and skills can lead to you obtaining that opportunity. You are able to inform your target audience of your knowledge and skills that are key to delivering on your value offering. If you are not able to do this, you do not have much of a chance of being selected for that opportunity. When you get that opportunity, be ready to apply your knowledge and skills to deliver your value offering.

PRACTICE

Choose a situation for this exercise. It can be your current position or one you may pursue in the future. Reflect on your value offering and all you learned from your experience and research to this point. What is the value you decided to offer? Identify the primary and complimentary knowledge and skills you consider important to your value offering. Then, identify the sources of information and methods of developing your knowledge and skills.

When you identify your requirements for developing your value offering, be specific. If you work in the legal profession and specialize in estate planning, do not simply say you want to know more about estate planning. There is a lot to estate planning. What specific facets do you want to learn? While you may accept that you want to know a lot more about it, identify the specifics you want to learn. You may choose to focus on learning more about how to help your clients limit estate taxes, how best to establish guardianships, preparation of wills, and other such specific elements of estate planning. Being specific will greatly aid you in identifying the right sources of information and methods of practice. You will also be better prepared to assess your progress in developing your knowledge and skills relevant to your value offering.

Also, be on the look-out for opportunities to refine your value offering. As you are conducting more research and practicing your desired skills, you may find other elements to include in your value offering. You may tweak how you crafted and defined it. You may have discovered something new to add. You may want to offer something different based on new-found interests or abilities. Re-assess to ensure you are on the track you want.

The form on the following page can help you organize this very important step. Expect to use multiple copies of this. Our list of knowledge and skills should be extensive.

Required Knowledge and Skills	Sources

- Ponder Page -

Chapter 6

It's Show Time!

Places everyone! Smiles! Dancing Shoes! It's show time!

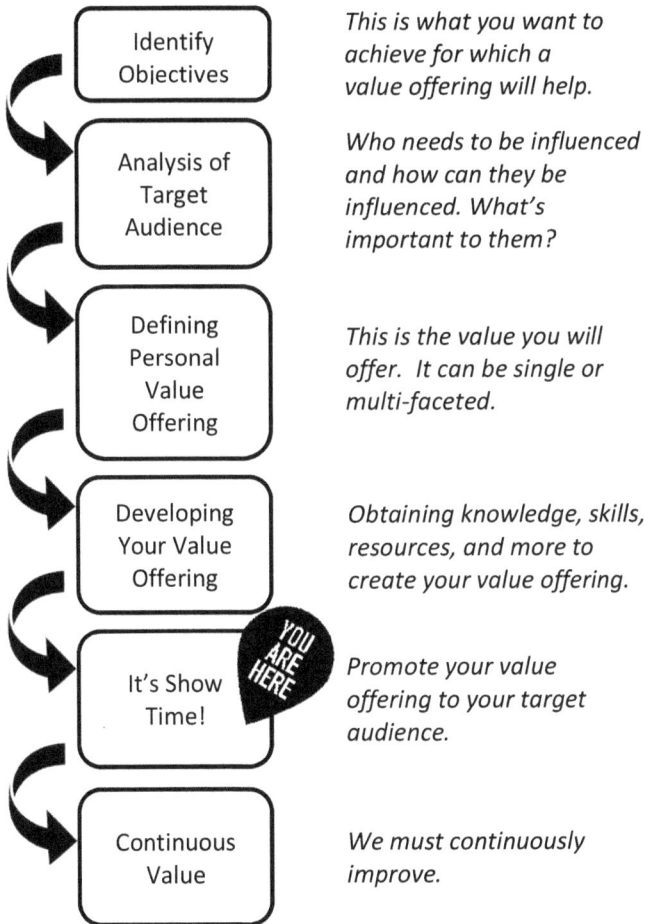

Identify Objectives	*This is what you want to achieve for which a value offering will help.*
Analysis of Target Audience	*Who needs to be influenced and how can they be influenced. What's important to them?*
Defining Personal Value Offering	*This is the value you will offer. It can be single or multi-faceted.*
Developing Your Value Offering	*Obtaining knowledge, skills, resources, and more to create your value offering.*
It's Show Time! (YOU ARE HERE)	*Promote your value offering to your target audience.*
Continuous Value	*We must continuously improve.*

We are going start with a lesson on the topic of *communicating*. The importance of good quality in communications has been recognized and taught for thousands of years. The sophists of ancient Greece – artifacts record this as far back as 2600 years ago – were teachers and many of them taught the topic of rhetoric (i.e., communications as it was commonly referred to at the time). Cicero in ancient Rome about 2200 years ago taught and wrote books on the topic of rhetoric. Many others did as well. I am certain the topic of communications was the topic of communications long before these teachers of communications.

Communications is not a new topic of teaching and learning. Yet, because it is so critical to civilized societies, it is a topic that warrants perpetual teaching and perpetual learning. There are countless books and classes on the topic. Teachers, coaches, and orators around the world try to help people with improving their communication skills. Even I have conducted training and consulting sessions on this important topic for many years. When communications are poor between speakers and receivers, receivers do not understand the speakers and the speakers do not understand the receivers. Without an understanding of what each party of a conversation is trying to explain, there is confusion and uncertainty. They will not be in a position to confidently make good decisions.

Communications is a complex topic that can take quite some time to cover. However, I am just going to focus on one thing that will help and that is *organization*. Organization in your communications is very important to getting your target audience to understand, appreciate, and trust in your value offering. To understand, to appreciate, and to trust.

Recall an instance where someone was talking to you and you listened for a while thinking, "what is he trying to say to me?". "My eyes are starting to gloss over." "I could use another cup of coffee about now." Each of us have plenty of these experiences. Have you ever asked, "What is your point?" "What is it that you're trying to tell me?" "And...your point is...?" We start asking these questions after listening to the person ramble for a long time, at least the patient people among us wait this long. Impatient people like myself will interrupt and ask the person to get to the point so I can help him and move on to my next project. That's me. This happens between co-workers, friends, family, everyone.

There are typically two causes of this problem of disorganization I mentioned above. One cause is that the speaker is speaking in a way that he understands without regard to the possibility the receiver may think differently or has a different level of understanding of the information. Sometimes the speaker is leaving out critical details that he has in his head and he does not acknowledge that the receiver does not have those details. Has that ever happened at home...? "Honey, I need more details and less pronouns, sorry. What? No, I cannot read your mind. Yes, I will work on that."

Fortunately, the setting in which we find ourselves presenting our value offering to someone can include people with similar experiences and knowledge. If you are a forensics specialist specializing in financial crimes and interviewing with a senior financial crimes law enforcement investigator, both of you speak the same language to some degree. You may not need to tailor your vernacular. You may not need to provide a lot of details to explain a trade craft both of you have.

Although, you may need to change how you speak if you are selling a product that your prospective customer has not seen nor heard of before now. If you are trying to sell a new topical antibiotic ointment to the average person, you are going to lose them if you start talking about cyclic polypeptide antibiotics like bacitracin zinc and neomycin and how they have bacteriostatic and bactericidal properties in preventing dephosphorylation of phospholipid carriers leading to bacterial cell lysis. You should convey your expertise and knowledge of your specialty, but form your presentation in a way that will be understood by your audience. If your audience does not understand you, you are not winning the game.

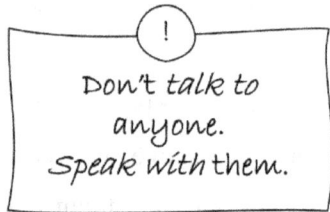

> !
> Don't talk to anyone.
> Speak with them.

The other common cause of this problem of disorganization – the receiver and speaker not understanding each other – is that the speaker resorts to providing information vice a message. This is a common mistake. A big mistake. Humans are sociable creatures. Most of us like to talk. But this is not the time for simply talking. It is a time for messaging. Big big big difference.

"I met my clients at the house yesterday. It needs work. One of the kitchen cabinet doors is broken. A bathroom faucet does not work. The fireplace is very dirty. My clients really like it, though. They are applying for a loan. The lender says they did not provide proof of employment yet. They have a son who plays soccer at the high school and may be playing tonight. I sent them an email and I spoke with the other Realtor. The seller does not want to lower their asking price. I need to pick up the kids from school today and Liz needs a haircut. We have an appointment at 6:00PM today. I have to go back to the house on Friday. When will you be home?"

Huh? I'm sorry, what are you saying? Is there something in there you need? What is your point...? Am I supposed to do something...?

There is a lot of information in there and I do not know whether or not the person sharing it with me wants me to do something with that information. Is there a problem with which I can help? Is there a point I should consider in my response? What is the message? There may not even be a message. Perhaps the person just wanted to chat. I need to understand! Do not just provide information. Provide your message, or messages. You can support your message with additional information, but please, please, please clearly provide your message so the receiver understands you.

When you are presenting your value offering, you need to do so with messages that help your target audience understand you. If they do not understand you, they may not want you and your value offering. Actually they may not be able to know whether or not they would want your value offering.

Informing people that you are an expert at yoga, that you have practiced yoga for ten years and you have been a yoga instructor for five years, that you have a 2,000 square foot studio, and your monthly price is $150 is just conveying information. That information likely pertains to many other yoga instructors and yoga studios. Why is being an instructor for five years important to your target audience? What about your facility being 2,000 square foot in size is important to your target audience? Why should a monthly price of $150 be important to your target audience? What is the reason the people you are meeting should become your students and not someone else's? What is the reason they should register with your studio now? What message or messages should you convey with this information?

You can start by letting your value offering speak for itself when it is well crafted and described. Your value offering may be something like *At my studio, you will always have the most enjoyable peaceful place to relax your mind and body with new friends.* I can dig that! Supplement your value offering with additional messages that embrace the information you want to share. Messages may include the following:

> ➤ You can reliability trust that you will receive the best experience with my high level of expertise and success record in helping yoga practitioners.
> ➤ You will be comforted and enjoy your yoga practice in my spacious and artfully decorated studio.
> ➤ You will save money and enjoy convenience with a monthly price that includes unlimited visits. Some nearby studios charge the same price and limit customers to only 4 visits.
> ➤ My prices are being discounted 10% for new registrations this month.

Start by identifying the messages you want to convey and select information that supports your information. That's the sequence. As a check on my effort to form messages, I review the information I want people to hear from me and I try to envision that person shrugging their shoulders at me and saying "why is that important to me?". The answer to that question is my message. This information I give you is important to you because it means *this to you*. Also, you may find that some of the information you initially decided to present does not support your messages and ought to be excluded. Or, that information may warrant a change in your message or messages.

I can tell someone that I know how to cook a lot of different dishes, but why is that important to them in considering me as their caterer for their family reunion. They only intend to buy one or two main dishes and a few side dishes, not my entire menu. They will not order everything I know how to cook. Ah, the message is that in selecting me they will have a large variety of options from which to choose in forming their menu. This gives them the opportunity to consider special diet restrictions of guests and to order a meal that is the favorite for many family members. That would contribute to an enjoyable family reunion.

When forming messages, determine what your target audience should consider as important about what you have to offer. Be ready to explain the reason or multiple reasons it is important. Do not just claim 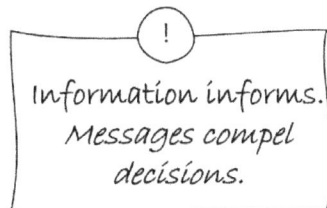 it to be important, be convincing. Consider the importance and the way you explain your messages in terms of relevant outcomes or achievements for the target audience. Your value offering is their value add.

The presentation flow is like this:

> *Value Offering* – Your succinct statement of the value you offer specifically for your target audience. Notice I say "specifically for" rather than "offer *to* your target audience". "Specifically for" infers relevancy.
>
> *Supporting Messages* – Depending on your situation, you may have one or several messages to convey. They provide more detail about your value offering in terms of value your target audience will receive. In other words, their benefit.
>
> *The Proof* – This is when you can finally provide that other information you have been wanting to share. Information you share should back up your claim to provide value as you presented in your value offering and supporting messages.

Here is an example used by a biology high school teacher.

Value Offering – I will enable each of my students to excel in their learning, in their preparation for college, and in their school attendance.

Message - I educate all of my students on the most current information available.

The Proof - I advance my proficiency on the discipline of biology with continuous education and research. I am an active member of the local

University's biological sciences forum. As a member of that forum, I write scholarly articles for their biology journal. I am a skilled biologist and educator.

Message - I adapt my teaching style to help students with their individualized needs.

The Proof - I recognize that students have differing learning styles. I am successful in providing one-on-one assistance, in using varying forms of presentations and class participation, and monitoring each student's progress. I meet individually with each student at the beginning of each class semester to assess their learning styles and other needs they may have.

Message - I connect with my students in ways to inspire them to fully participate and maximize their potential at school.

The Proof - My students readily engage with me during class and, when needed, after class for additional instruction. My students have been eager to participate in class and school projects and activities. My students routinely have the highest attendance record at the school. Some of my higher performing students enthusiastically avail themselves to help other students.

Message - I am a team player, highly capable and fully committed to participating in school-wide requirements in areas of academics, extra-

curricular programs, management, and other requirements to help the
school on the whole.

The Proof - I collaborate with fellow science teachers and school
administrators in efforts to continuously improve education for our
students. I have contributed to developing creative school activities to
help my students. I actively participate with the PTO to work closing with
parents of our students.

There will be times when your target audience has a different interest
than you. They may be looking for something different than what you
initially offer. They are looking for something else that they consider
important. They may be right in looking for whatever they seek and
having less interest in what you offer. Recall us previously talking about
how important it is to try to understand your target market when defining
your value offering and preparing for your presentation? You may still
have an opportunity. In this situation, look for ways that your value
offering can compliment or in some way help your target audience with
what they seek. Just because there is a little difference between you and
your target audience does not mean there is no good match between the
two of you. Also, sometimes they may not have considered what you have
to offer and, as a result, have not considered its value yet. It is possible
that they could benefit more from your offering and they may understand
that if you properly communicate. With what? Messages! Look for
synergies among everyone's interests and bridge the gap.

PRACTICE

By this point of the process, forming your messages and proof points should be decently easy. You have your value offering crafted and defined, and now you are adding more detail for presenting it to your target audience.

Write down your value offering. Identify multiple messages. If you come up with only one, continue looking for more. You may find that the one message you identified actually includes multiple messages, each of which can be broken out. Remember, messages describe your value offering in more detail on how you will deliver. Then add the information that supports your claims in those messages. Much of this information you would have identified much earlier, yet continue looking for more if needed.

Use the following form to help organize this project. Conduct this practice in a group or at least have another person contribute input. This is a phase that benefits well from good input.

Value Offering	
Message 1	
Proof	
Message 2	
Proof	
Message 3	
Proof	

Message 4	
Proof	
Message 5	
Proof	

- Ponder Page -

Chapter 7

Good, Better, Best

Have you heard someone say "you're never too old to learn" or "we are always learning"? We probably heard this more times than we wish we had. The message is very important, though, because it is true that we should continuously improve. That is how we continue to provide value to others and to ourselves.

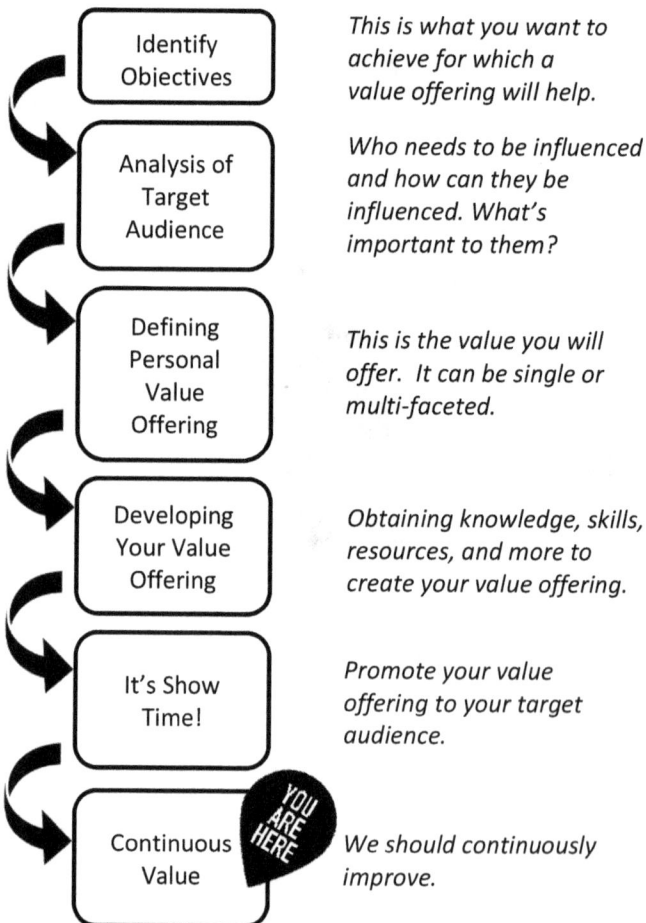

Step	Description
Identify Objectives	*This is what you want to achieve for which a value offering will help.*
Analysis of Target Audience	*Who needs to be influenced and how can they be influenced. What's important to them?*
Defining Personal Value Offering	*This is the value you will offer. It can be single or multi-faceted.*
Developing Your Value Offering	*Obtaining knowledge, skills, resources, and more to create your value offering.*
It's Show Time!	*Promote your value offering to your target audience.*
Continuous Value	*We should continuously improve.*

YOU ARE HERE

The world around us changes. People change. Technology changes. Knowledge changes. Society changes. The one thing that is constant is change. (We have heard that cliché, too.) We are great today and our value offering is a winner for prime time. Yet as changes occur in our surroundings, we may need to tweak our value offering to maintain or even increase its relevancy. In face of change our value offering may still be a great value offering, but changes around us lead to new expectations for what we should offer.

We are really good at performing public administration roles. In the city's Planning Department, we excel at managing the Master Plan, understanding construction materials, applying building codes and zoning ordinances, processing customer service inquiries, record keeping, and budget management. Materials used in building homes and commercial buildings, paving roads, and underground sewer systems change. The way new paving materials are used to divert rain water and to decrease icing change. Building codes change to make us safer in our homes and businesses. Our communities grow and need changes to roads, parking lots, traffic signals, and public amenities. Our value offering may have been great 10 years ago, but is it as great as it should be today in view of so many changes in our community. Another cliché – have you heard someone speak to "keeping with the times"? When the world around us is updated, we keep up with the times or we become outdated. Stay up to date or be out of date.

I frequently incorporate the concept of *continuous performance improvement* in my consultations. Many of you may be familiar with *continuous process improvement* which is a common term. I much prefer the word *performance* because it specifically refers to the central matter. A process can be improved without performance being improved. Performance includes a standard and that standard is defined by the people involved. Improving performance can include improving processes, training and skill development, motivation and mindset, and much more. To grow, to continue being great in our changing world, we must consider continuously improving our performance.

I do not suggest you be dissatisfied with your performance today if it does not meet today's standards when your performance was great yesterday in view of yesterday's standards. All of us should understand there is a relative nature to this. We are great today for today's standards, and we will be great tomorrow. But, will we be great *enough* tomorrow for tomorrow's standards? Be able to adapt and grow. Be visionary and proactive in readying for tomorrow's requirements. You will be able to prepare to tackle tomorrow's changes and to learn from them.

In every role I had, I was committed to excellence. I did not always perform well, but I definitely tried. Fortunately, I have a good track record and I had many bosses who complimented me a lot. I was selected for a number of senior positions and for very exciting opportunities. I also have many *learning experiences*. We – all – do. My track record did not improve until I understood and embraced having a value offering.

As you pursue continuous performance improvement, I recommend taking the following approach.

1. *Assess your performance outcomes in relation to the performance requirements placed on you.* If you are supposed to manage a program within 1% of budget, either over or under, and you are managing it at 3% over, this is performance you may assess as low. This may be an opportunity to excel. Be realistic, though. Not all disparities are problematic. Focus on the ones that really need attention.

2. *Identify potential contributors to your performance outcome and categorize them by "personal" and "public" contributors.* Personal contributors are those that you present such as your own knowledge and skills, motivation, personally owned resources, and personal behavior. Public contributors essentially come from anyone else such as an organization's policies and operations processes, behaviors and decisions of other people, environments, and resources provided by someone other than you. The way you manage your daily schedule or track or do not track deadlines can be a personal contributor. Not having an operational printer in your office because the IT team has not fixed it is the result of a public contributor – the IT team has not fixed it. (Hopefully you are not on that IT team…)

Sometimes there will be a relationship between personal and public contributors. For example, the way you manage your work schedule can be a personal contributor yet that boss who thrives on scheduling far too many meetings is a public contributor. There is clearly a relationship between the two and you need to address both of them.

3. *Identify potential approaches to improving or overcoming the contributors, and implement them.* When working on the personal contributors, refer to the approaches you took to initially form your value offering. It is the same. You will research, practice, and ask for input. Work collaboratively to address the public contributors. You may be able to foster change in the public contributors. You may also discover that they are fine and the need for change resides with your personal contributors. Keep an open mind to all of this.

4. *Measure and re-assess.* Monitor your performance and look for changes in the outcomes. This step is what makes performance improvement continuous – Continuous Performance Improvement.

Do not change just to change. There can be a lot of pressure on us to do better all the time. Even I am adding some pressure with my guidance in this book. Honestly, though, sometimes we are great just as we are. We meet the requirements and in some cases we excel. I have seen far too many managers tell their teams that they want them to always learn, to always strive to be better, and to do more while they fail to recognize how great their team already is. I have done some of that, too, in this book. Change to improve where improvement is necessary. If the change would not add value or in some way make things better, then you risk disrupting the great performance you already have. Ensure any changes you implement are necessary and relevant.

Continuous performance improvement is a cycle. We perform, we assess, we improve, we perform, we assess, we improve. For long term success, we need continuous performance improvement. Consider those really good athletes. When they first started playing their sport, they did not stop there. They continue to train, assess themselves, and train some more in an effort to improve their performance. Their performance and the effort for continuous performance improvement are part of their value offering to the team just like your performance is part of your value offering to your place of work, to your customers, to any number of other people.

Here is another scenario. Likely all of us have experiences calling a support team (help desk). We may have issues with our IT equipment, a purchase, the software on our computer, our phone or TV services. The support provided is typically categorized by tiers. When I formed or oversaw support teams, it was common to categorize level of support in multiple tiers ranging from "0" up to "4", sometimes as many as "6". Tier 0 support was often what individuals could handle on their own such as resetting their own passwords or downloading information. Tier 1 was that initial level of support that involved engagement by a customer (i.e., a caller) and a member of the support team where that support team member was able to resolve the issue. Tier 2 required escalation to a specialized team, and so on.

I witnessed many instances where the support sought by a customer was easily Tier 1 support, yet the support team was unable to help. The support team member would be caught off guard by not having an answer and they had to call on a manager or other expert for additional assistance. Customers either waited a long time for help or did not receive any solution to their issues.

What could this team do? They could start by identifying the customer issues that had low resolution rate and train on solutions. (A resolution rate is the number of trouble tickets resolved within prescribed standards compared to the total number of trouble tickets received.) The team could be better resourced with reference materials so team members would have ready access to important information and no need to call on other people for help. The team could replace some of its members. The team could be kept updated and trained on new components being installed and provided to users. Depending on the personal and public contributors, there could be any number of potential approaches to continuously improving the team's value offering and, thus, their performance.

PRACTICE

Consider your current role and all its performance requirements. Are you required to meet deadlines? Produce a certain amount of product? Develop an operations plan for your nationwide stores? Achieve a specific customer service feedback score? Follow-up with customers within a specified time after providing them a service? All of us have standards placed upon us in our current roles. I have never met anyone who achieved all of them, including me. Seriously. After decades of serving in senior positions and having multiple clients – small and very large clients – I have worked with so many people I can't count that high. Do not feel bad when you identify some shortcomings. In fact, I would be concerned if someone told me they did not have any. Be honest with yourself. When we are honest with ourselves, we keep the door open to learning more. This is the reason we are studying this topic of crafting and improving our value offering.

Choose one of the shortcomings you identified. Hide the rest away for later. No one needs to know about them now. What is that shortcoming? Ensure you can describe it. Maybe you can quantify it with numbers. It does not matter whether it is chronic or something that happened for a brief moment. If there was a shortcoming, something contributed to it and it may occur again.

What are the contributors? Which ones are personal and which ones are public? Be detailed in how you describe the contributors. With more detail, you set yourself up to fully understand them and then address them. Do not just say you forgot something and that led to missed deadlines. We are working on our value offering. So, a contributor would not be something like forgetting about deadlines, if missing deadlines was a shortcoming you identified. Forgetting deadlines is a symptom of a contributor or contributors. The contributors may be more like failing to effectively track tasks, agreeing to quick-turn deadlines without properly determining the amount of effort and time needed for the projects, or being easily distracted.

How do you fix the contributors? Hint: *I don't know* or *someone else got in my way so it's their problem* are not the right answers. Regardless of whether we introduced our own contributors or other people contributed to our performance challenges, we own the situation. It is our performance, we own it. Consider training, re-engineering processes, changing policy, collaborating with others on behaviors, different tactics in communications, changing your approach to time management and work schedule, redefining roles, and so on and so on. You may likely find that multiple approaches can and should be applied to individual contributors. You may also need to apply a phased approach where you implement some solutions early and follow with some additional solutions later that rely on the first ones to be completed.

Finally, identify a schedule for re-assessing. Provide enough time for changes to produce results. Only you and your team will know how much time is needed or how much time can be afforded. When the results are good, celebrate and keep up the good work. When the results are not as good as intended, you may need to either implement different approaches to addressing the contributors or change the way you implemented the other approaches.

Try using the following form to guide you through this process.

Shortfall	Contributors	Personal or Public	Approach to Addressing the Shortfalls	Timeline for Re-Assessment

- Ponder Page -

Chapter 8

May There Be Many Successes

You are valuable. I know you will have many successes. You have value to offer and it is important that you continue improving upon it. You have had many experiences in life and each of them was a learning opportunity. There will be many more. Take it all in. Gather it all together in your value bundle.

Be motivated. Be committed. Be persistent. You are on the right track. This really is a journey, so keep moving. The world around us is moving, so we must keep moving, too.

Keep this guide close by. Review it and reflect upon the guidance I shared. There are many books and other resources written by people who want to help us improve. I encourage reading more of them and gleaning what you find in each of them that works best for you. Put it into practice and adapt where needed to fit your needs.

I sincerely hope that with this book I have been able to help you. I hope my guidance helps you a lot. I wish you good luck in all you do and much enjoyment in your current and yet-to-be achieved successes.

About The Author – Ron Pieper

Ron Pieper has been providing self-improvement training and consulting services for clients, customers, colleagues, and his own teams for over three decades.

During his 37-years of service in the United States Navy and the Federal Government, as a business executive and consultant, Ron held many leadership positions in which he studied and placed into practice self-improvement initiatives in areas of leadership, operational performance, business operations, business planning and strategy, organization development, value offering, marketing, and many more. He developed and implemented training programs and consulted for several large and small business, Government organizations, and individuals.

He defined his many career roles to provide service to many other people. His current endeavors are likewise focused on service. Service in helping people be the best they can be is his commitment. This is his passion. He continues to serve and is now providing his assistance in book form to reach more people.

Ron holds a Masters of Science in Organizational Leadership and a Graduate Certificate in Non-Profit Leadership. His research, learning, and service continue.

www.ingramcontent.com/pod-product-compliance
Lightning Source LLC
Chambersburg PA
CBHW070813290326
41931CB00011BB/2208